Miles Walker Art Book Nine

The paintings in this book are otherworldly art, strange but not unfamiliar. We are limited, not by our abilities, but by our vision. I believe the visual arts should reflect the lifestyle of its culture and period. I am convinced that different people you know bring out different sides in all of us. I have spent most of my life as an art director in advertising, doing a job I love and therefore I feel I have never had to work a day in my life.

Art Book 9

Miles Walker Art Book Nine (artbook 9)

© Copyright 2019 Miles Walker

Book 9 in the Art Book Series. All rights reserved. mileswalker.com

No part of this book may be reproduced in any form or by any means without permission in writing from the author.

© Copyright: All original illustrations, paintings and drawings in this book are by Miles Walker.

Any quotes are the copyright of the original author.

Other books by the author: Synthetic Sea Sixty Six, After Age, Uani, Themus, Soft Journey, Paradise Papers, Doodles & Dreams. Miles Walker's Diary. Miles Walker's Dictionary. Miles Walker's Doodles. Miles Walker's Artworks. Miles Walker's Artisus. Miles Walker Surreal Art. Miles Walker's Artxtra. Miles Walker Artfully Surreal.

Typefaces: Cracked thanks Apple. Bitner.....Thanks Jonathan Hill, Northern Block, I just luv it at 150 horizontal scale. Hiroshige.....Thanks Cynthia Hollandsworth Batty for this font which I have used so much over the years......Xenu from the type king Ray Larrabie.....Some Optima and Compacta from the sixties and seventies!...Rub me down Letraset you were the edge then.

This is a work of fiction. Drawings, paintings, doodles, characters, names, places, events and incidents are either the products of the author's imagination or used in a fictitious manner. Any resemblance to actual persons, living or dead, or actual events is purely coincidental.....

The views and opinions expressed and described or contained in this book are fiction and not the views of the artist/author Miles Walker.

The author and publisher have made every effort to ensure that the information in this book was correct at press time, the author and publisher do not assume and hereby disclaim any liability to any party for any loss, damage, or disruption caused by errors or omissions, whether such errors or omissions result from negligence, accident, or any other cause.

www.mileswalker.com
or email: mswalkers@gmail.com or dandg@portal.ca

Miles Walker Art Book Nine

No matter how you look at it, life these days is strange. Millions of Facebook users had their profiles hijacked 2016, then 2018, 500 million had their Facebook information compromised.....Technology is the arranging of life so that one need not experience it. Zuckered.....What a mind blowing concept. Let your avatar join us. Information warfare and cyber crime is going to interfere with your personal identity. War does not determine who is right, only who is left.

Strange as it may still seem my life is based on a true story.....Encore, I was out of my mind when he told me I was a puncshuarion.....This is my journal of current surreal visual art ideas delivered in pixels, this book is an imagination construction kit. Please note this is a Picture Book so the words are not to be taken seriously, they are 101 Word Lite!!! A picture is worth a thousand words.....My artwork and philosophical search is a constant effort at wondering critically about facial recognition and everything else I see around me. Better late than never, but never late is better.....Laughter is Life's best Tranquiliser with no side effects. Enjoy.

pre facial recognition

When you look through this book you will be face to face with so many of my portraits of people, their lines of life, their family character, handed down genetically, showing their hardships and happiness…..Now just spend a few minutes and go and look in the mirror, who are you? A facial recognition system is a technology capable of identifying or verifying a person from a digital image or a video source. There are multiple methods in which facial recognition systems work, but in general, they work by comparing selected facial features from a given image with faces within a database. It is also described as a Biometric Artificial Intelligence based application that can uniquely identify a person by analysing patterns based on the person's facial textures and shape. Lets face it crime detection is helped by facial recognition. So look at the pictures in this book, put on your best face to impress…..But remember we all wear masks.

Sometimes you just know time is a great teacher,
but unfortunately it kills all its students.....

I found out at your funeral (picture above 39 years and 79 years) you had developed twenty nine skyscrapers in three countries, planted a teak forest in Thailand and lived the winter decembers in Marina di Ragusa in Sicily.

Behind Bowen Island, Howe Sound, British Columbia, Canada.

Open AI, soon they will know what you are thinking.....
GPT2 is this the computer programme writing this book
and putting in my favourite spelling mistakes? How much
will they let me think and see when I am 93?

Rodney inspired me to paint the pictures that are in this gallery
hallway, which are shown in more detail on page 222 and 216.

Abstraction and Chaos.....Don't ask. What are we doing here?

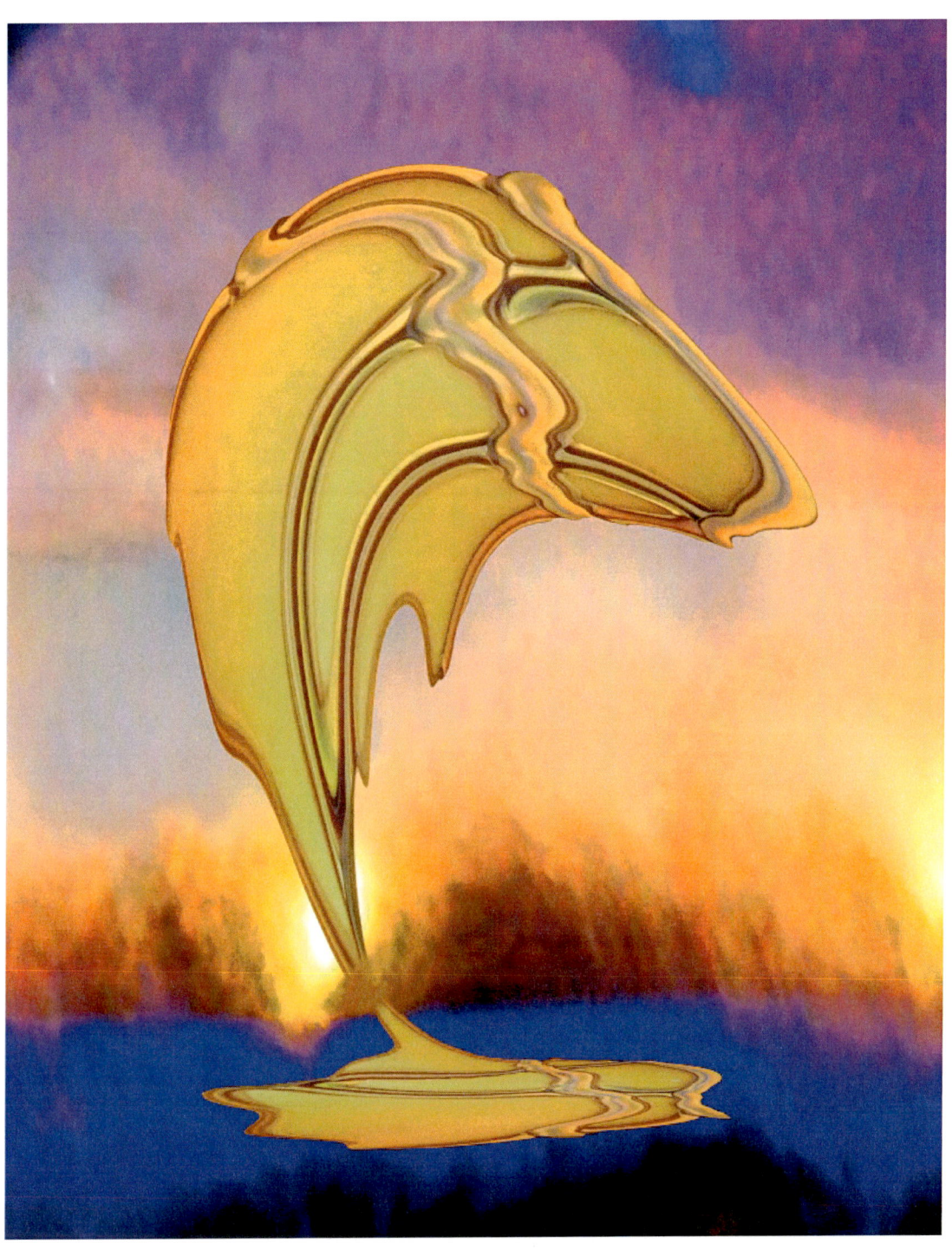

You know neural networks will learn to create themselves.

Eebe from Wadeeebrige, rite boy, father from Trebetherick. He is a wanker and skives, now sells houses and boats in St Ives.....

Hey.....The meaning of life is to pass it on.....Oral sandpaper is real dire rear.

Hypnagogic blue dream baby.....Introduce yourself to the space time between semi-lucid sleep state..... During sleep onset, a window of opportunity arises in the form of hypnagogia, a semi-lucid sleep state where we all begin dreaming before we fall fully unconscious. So sleeping is unconscious? Hypnagogia is characterised by phenomenological unpredictability, distorted perception of space and time and spontaneous, fluid idea association. Dalí, Tesla, Edison and Poe each accessed this state by napping with a steel ball in hand to capture creative ideas generated in hypnagogic microdreams when it dropped to the floor below. This system enables future research into sleep, an underutilised and understudied state of mind vital for memory, learning and creativity.

You cannot unsee things but you can over time try to forget them.

Never forget what is worth remembering or remember what is best forgotten.

I have tried to paint my soul pancake, but buttermilk in a dream is so hard to find.

Kanaka Bay, West Coast, Canada.

Children are Hope.....Body language speaks louder than words.

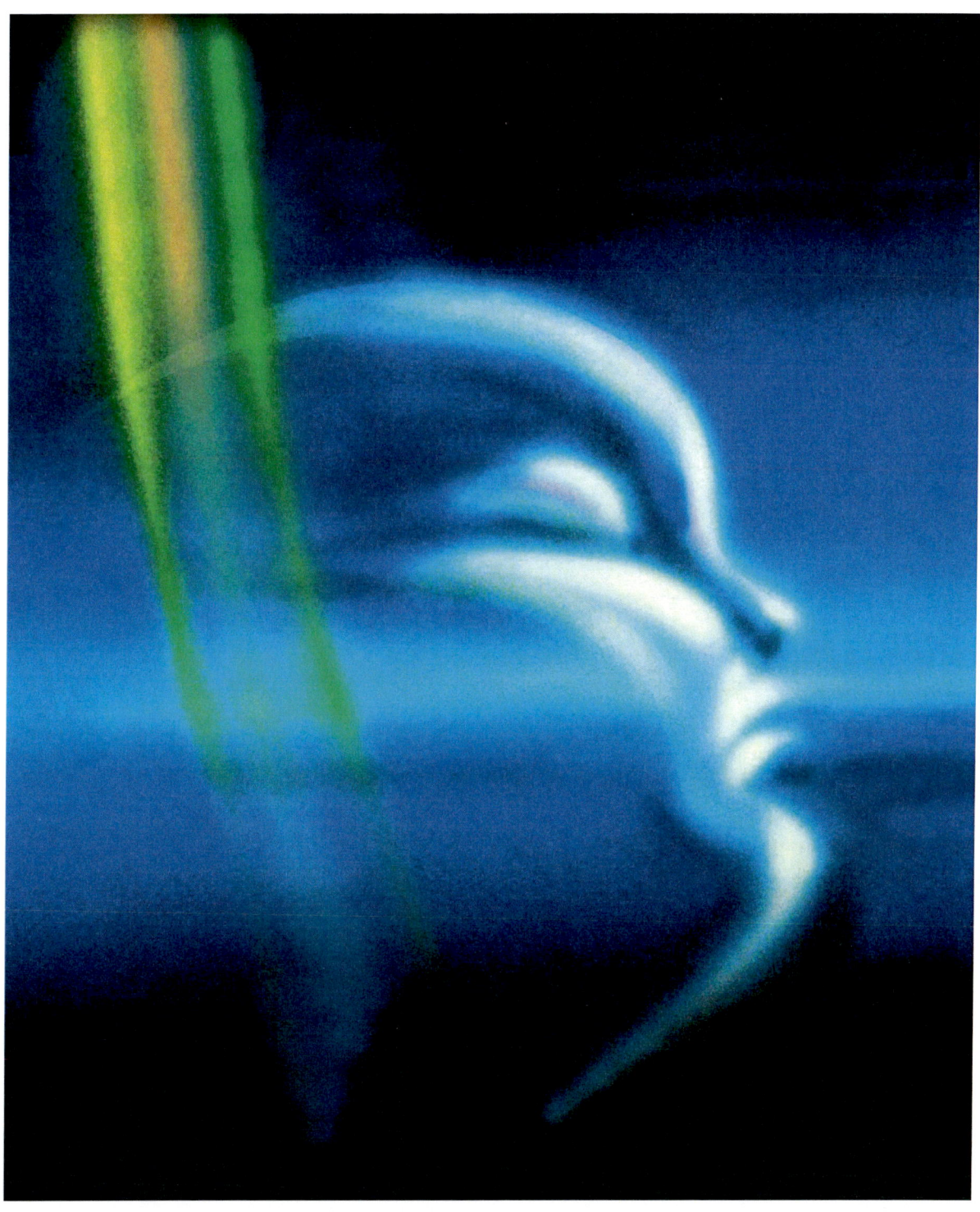

Don't feel blue because Today is Yesterday's Tomorrow......Maybe not if you are in the TARDIS.

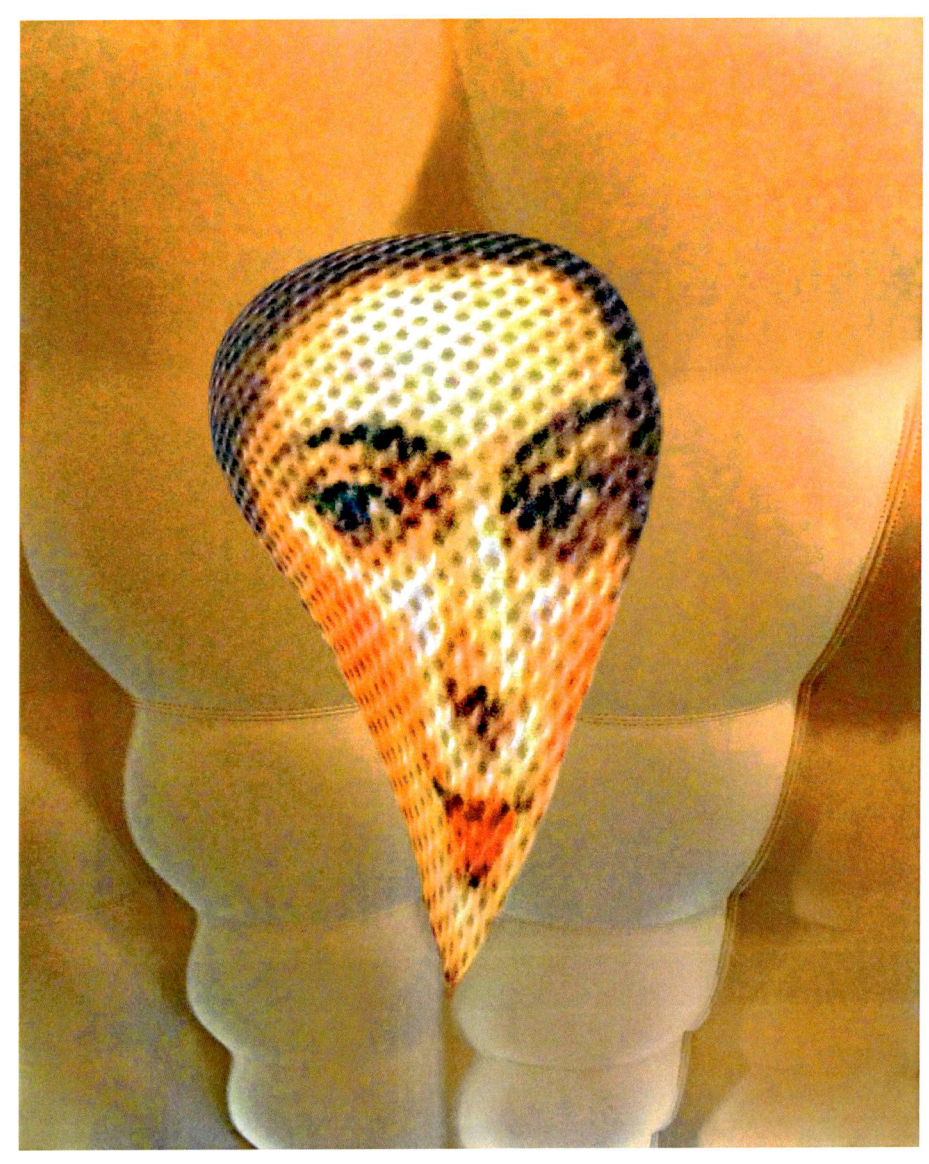

I should do something about my life.....Maybe tomorrow!

Conjunctivitis.com — "that's a site for sore eyes."
You may well laugh but Humans are moving into a minefield of unknowables.

We have changed dramatically from the agricultural, industrial and information revolution…..Machine learning, AI engineering, bio-genetics are the start of the next revolution, very soon we will have the power to change humanity.

In a heated discussion most of us know how to say nothing; few of us know when.

Legs.....Of all the things you wear, your expression is the most important.

Modafinil.....The world's first safe smart drug.....Lets make you concentrate.
The way you experience the world is not the way it is.....
Abstract yes/no can you see it?

28 Humankind, despite its artistic pretensions, its sophistication, and its many accomplishments.....

Owes its existence to a six-inch layer of topsoil and the fact that it rains!

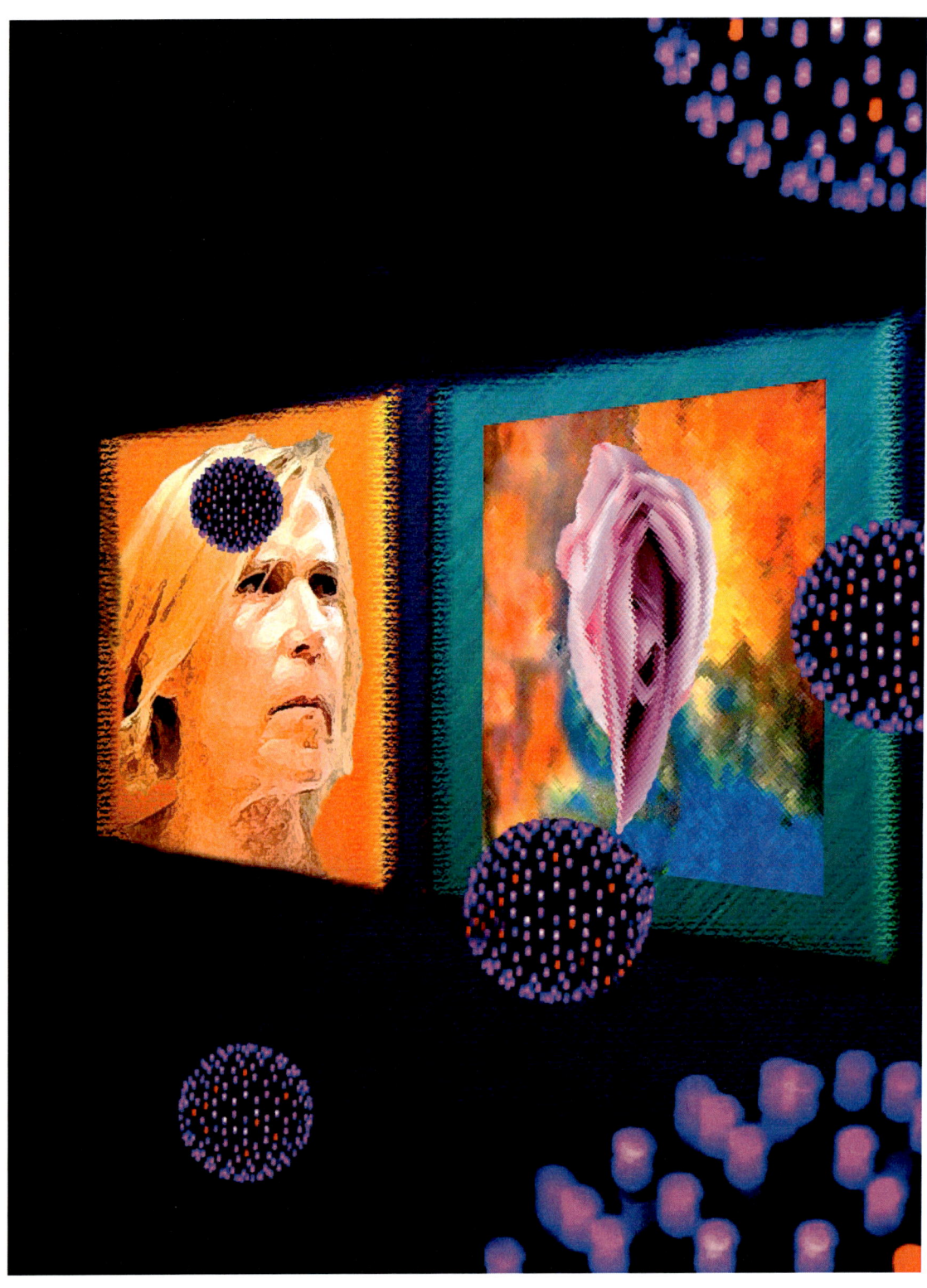

Love is not a perfect match, it is the connection between two people. If it were as simple as pairing up people who are most alike, the work would be easy.

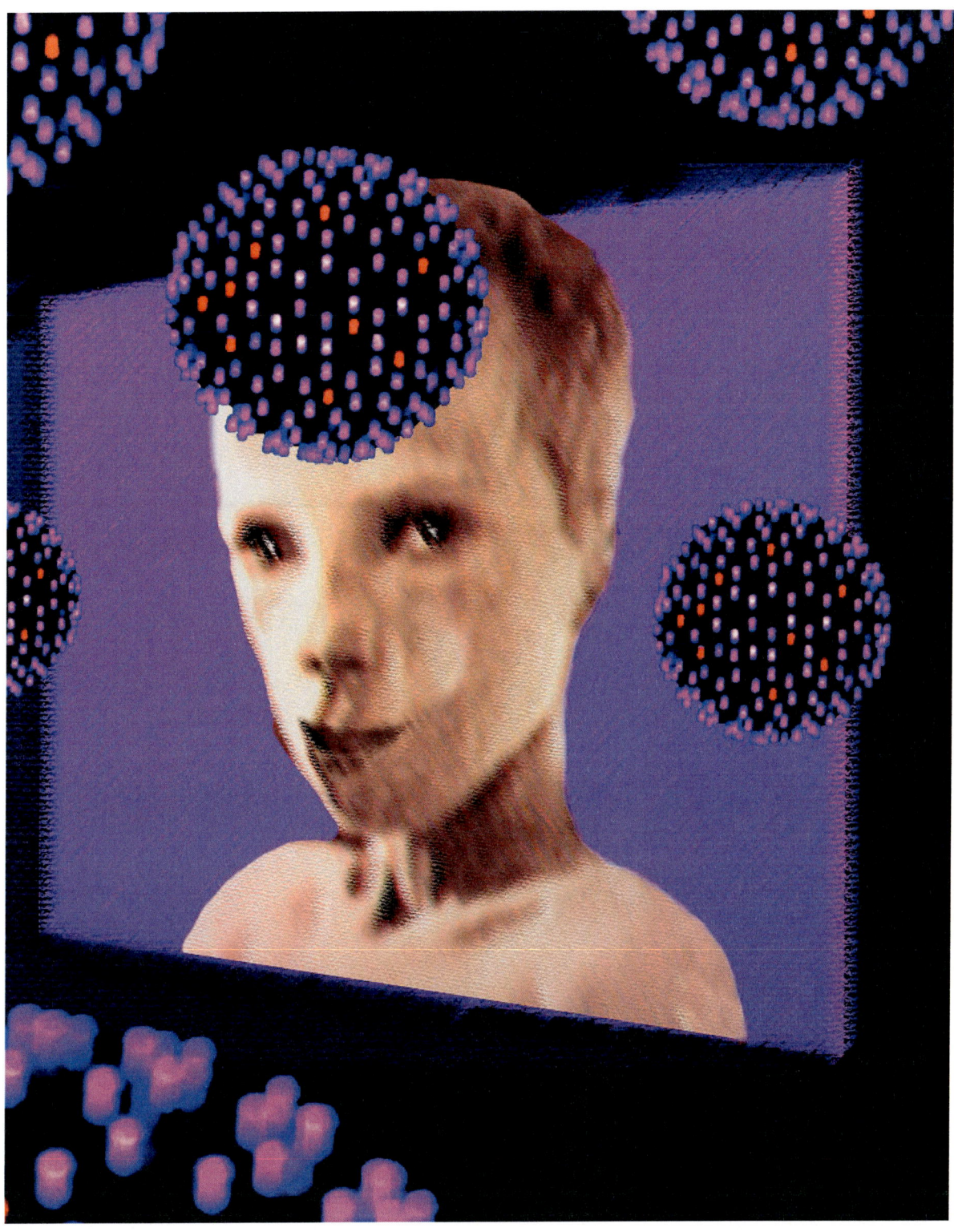

We are not searching for our perfect partners, we are searching for the kind of unexplainable connection that defies logic and reason and timing and sense.

We live as long as we're remembered.

Mind watch, this picture trips the light fantastic and travels into a seventy year old brain.....
Strange how much you've got to know before you know how little you know......Please look at
the centre of it for sixty seconds. No blinking lightly.....

How many people do you know that have seen one?

Don't you love the satisfaction and extra excitement you feel when you think life is really working for you.....No one can take that away from you.

Kernow Estuary, misty sunrise.....Feathering for mackerel on high tide swells.

Red Moon Rising, Lunacy rules.....I don't suffer from insanity. I enjoy every minute of it.

A man can fail many times, but he isn't a failure until he gives up.

In the 1960s, people took acid to make the world weird. Now the world is weird, and people take Prozac to make it normal.

Just one of a hundred and twenty nine things that do not add up to now, Leviticus 18.22 System error reboot.

We have the illusion of choice when we vote, politics is about money. We are all repressed prisoners in the rules we live by……

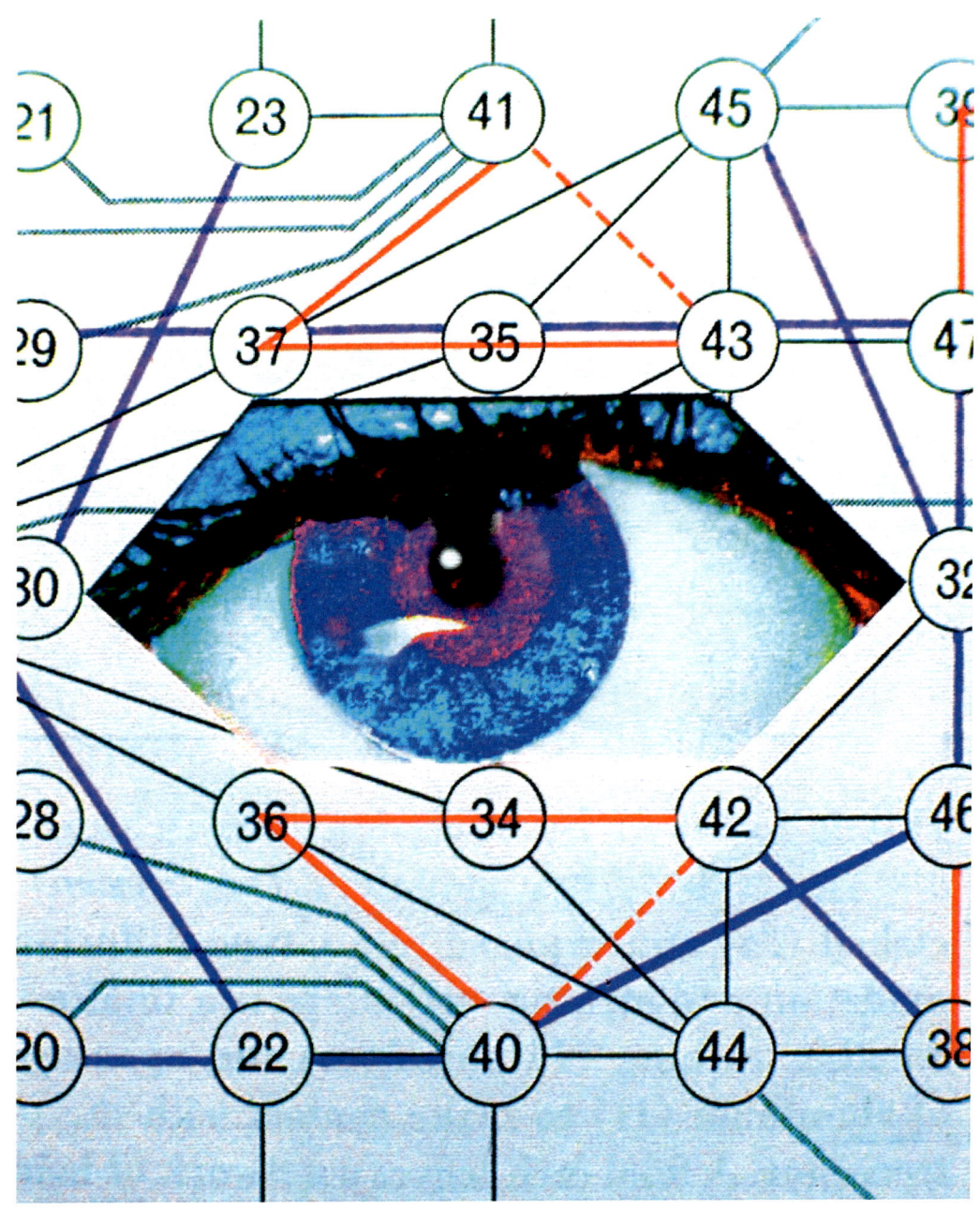

Constipated mathematicians can work it out with a pencil and paper.....Butt birthdays are good for you.....Research has shown that the more you have, the longer you live.....

If only we could understand nature, so many problems would be solved.
If insect losses cannot be halted it will be catastrophic for the survival of
biological humans and earth's ecosystem.

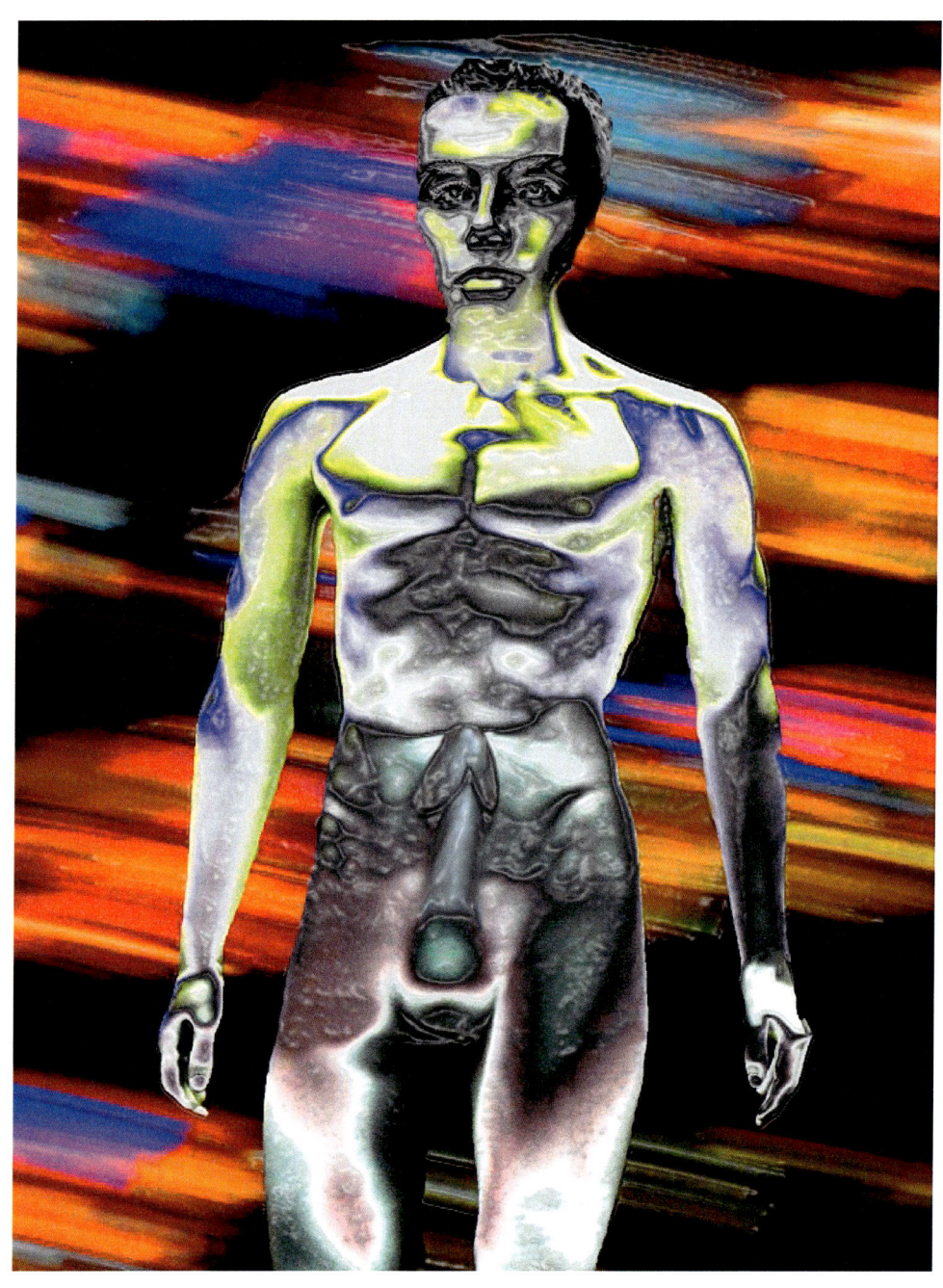

People who think they know it all are especially annoying to those of us who do. All my friends before 1980 should be photoshopped.....

Have you ever looked at your X and wondered Y.....Relationships are a lot like algebra!!!

Your clear conscience is the first sign of a bad memory. Our thoughts reveal the beliefs we have about ourselves.....

Her Doppelganger lived in a ring of fire. She swims through silk sheets when wakefullness takes her.....She can still enjoy those few moments when waking. On the new journey all seven billion will be exterminated!

War is a great way to control resources and markets and employs so many people and makes good money for manufacturers.

Life is a beach..... I just miss the way it used to be..... "I tried to look up impotence on the Internet, but nothing came up." Everything means nothing if we have a nuclear war or major nuclear accident.....

My mystery socks are David . . . .? To understand take
one of these tablets orally see page 207.

An artist is not one who has solved life's problems. He is one who accepts life's problems.

My year keeps turning into something different than I planned.....

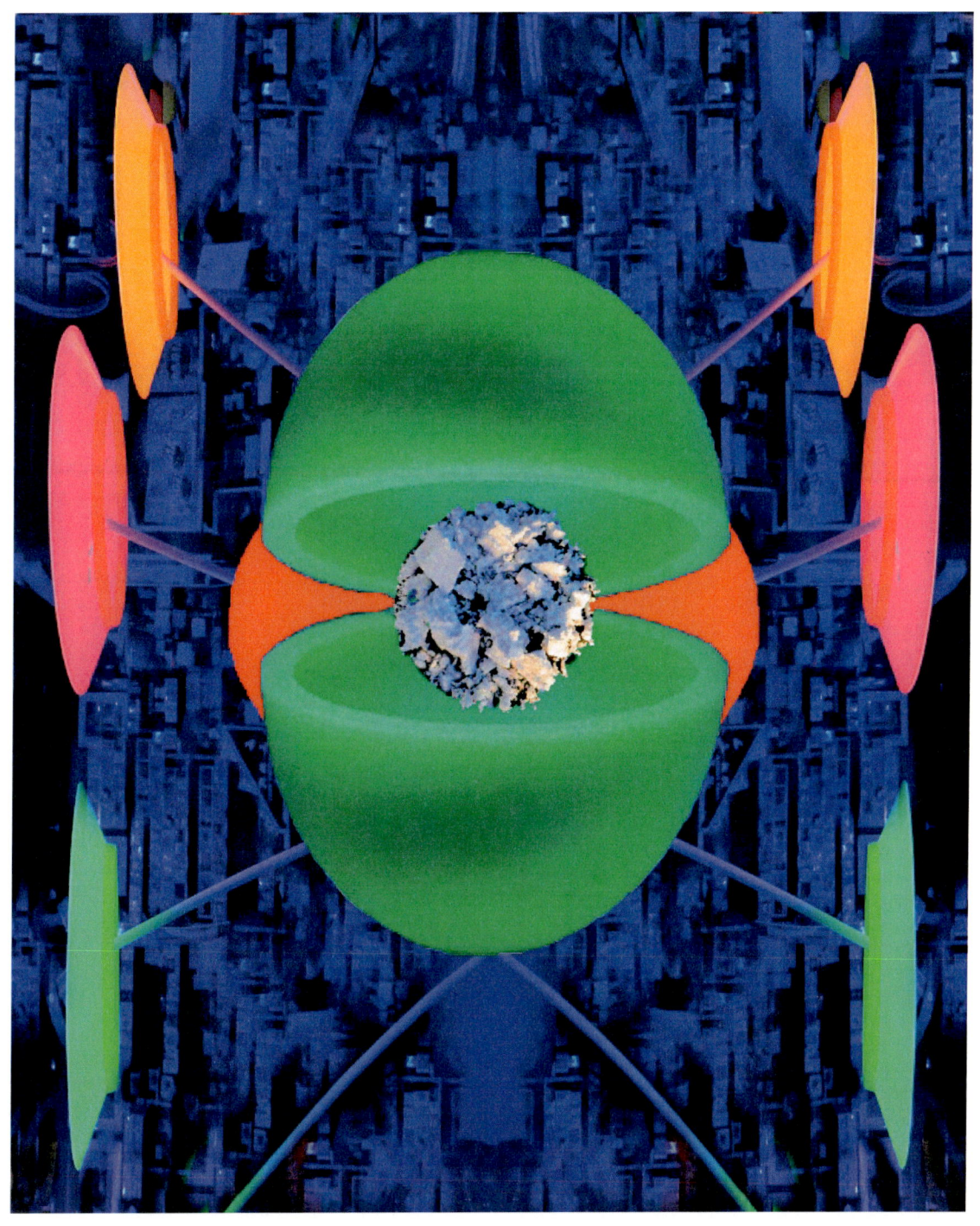

Edgar was right when he said "Art is not what you see, but what you make others see".....

What does it take to create consciousness? A curious mind? Look at the footprint left by Neil Armstrong, that could not happen at the temperature of 245 F it has to have moisture to make that impression.

Living in Canada's Lotus Land.....Thinking out of the box.....You must know and understand why, how, when, and where your box was created to know how to go beyond it.

Pattern and chaos – the real meaning of the future.

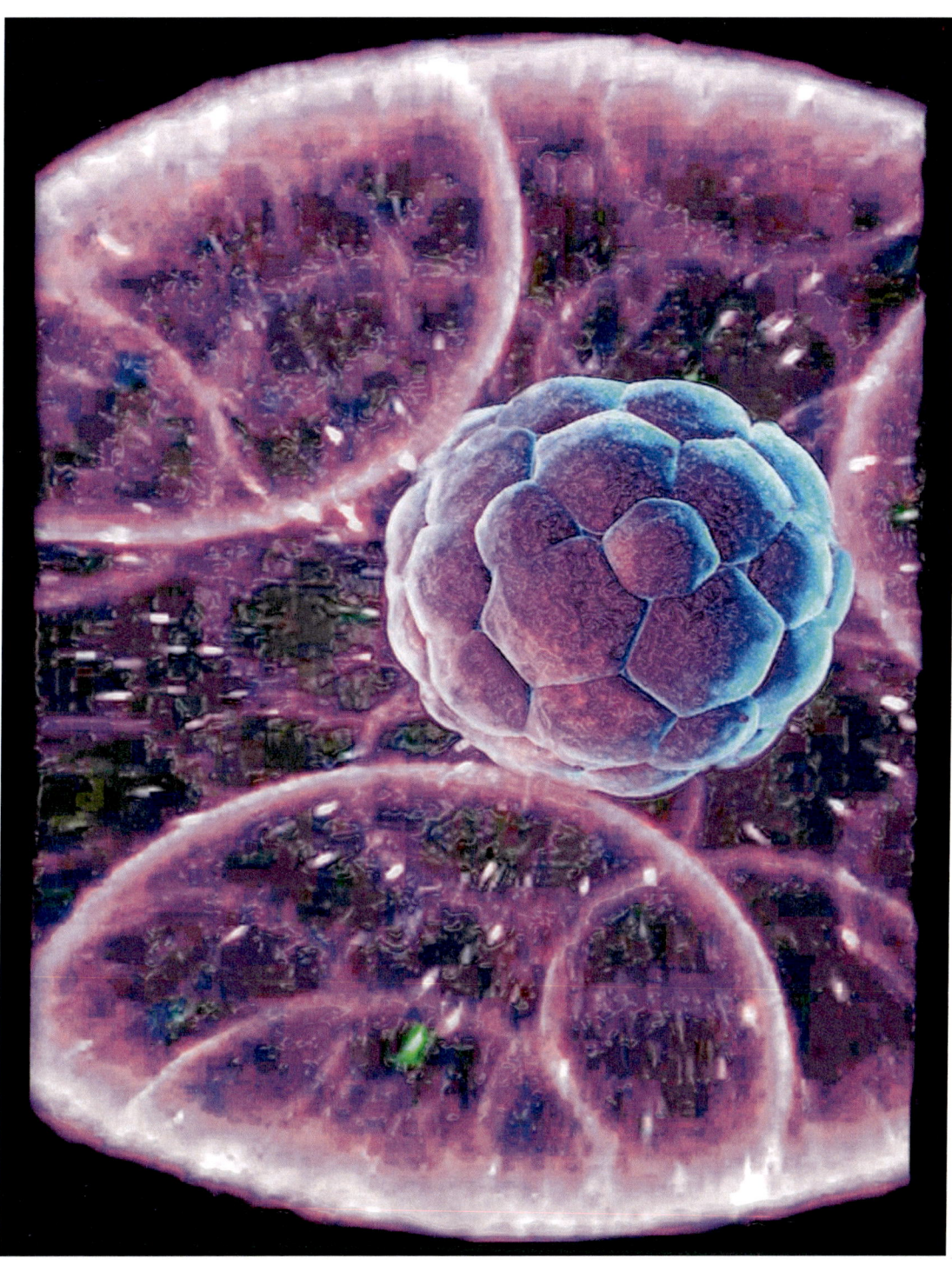

We can now grow the right kind of people, none of this intercourse and waiting 9 months.

Your wish changes nothing. Your decision and action changes everything....You are fit!

Preserve a shadow every day, as on the other side you will enjoy the energy of light.

The real world is the material matter.....Time, space and matter are primary.

I am my life's luggage of all my experiences and memories.....So colour me orange.....

The hills are alive with the sound of.....

.....Talking talking T A L K I N G Tuscan trees.

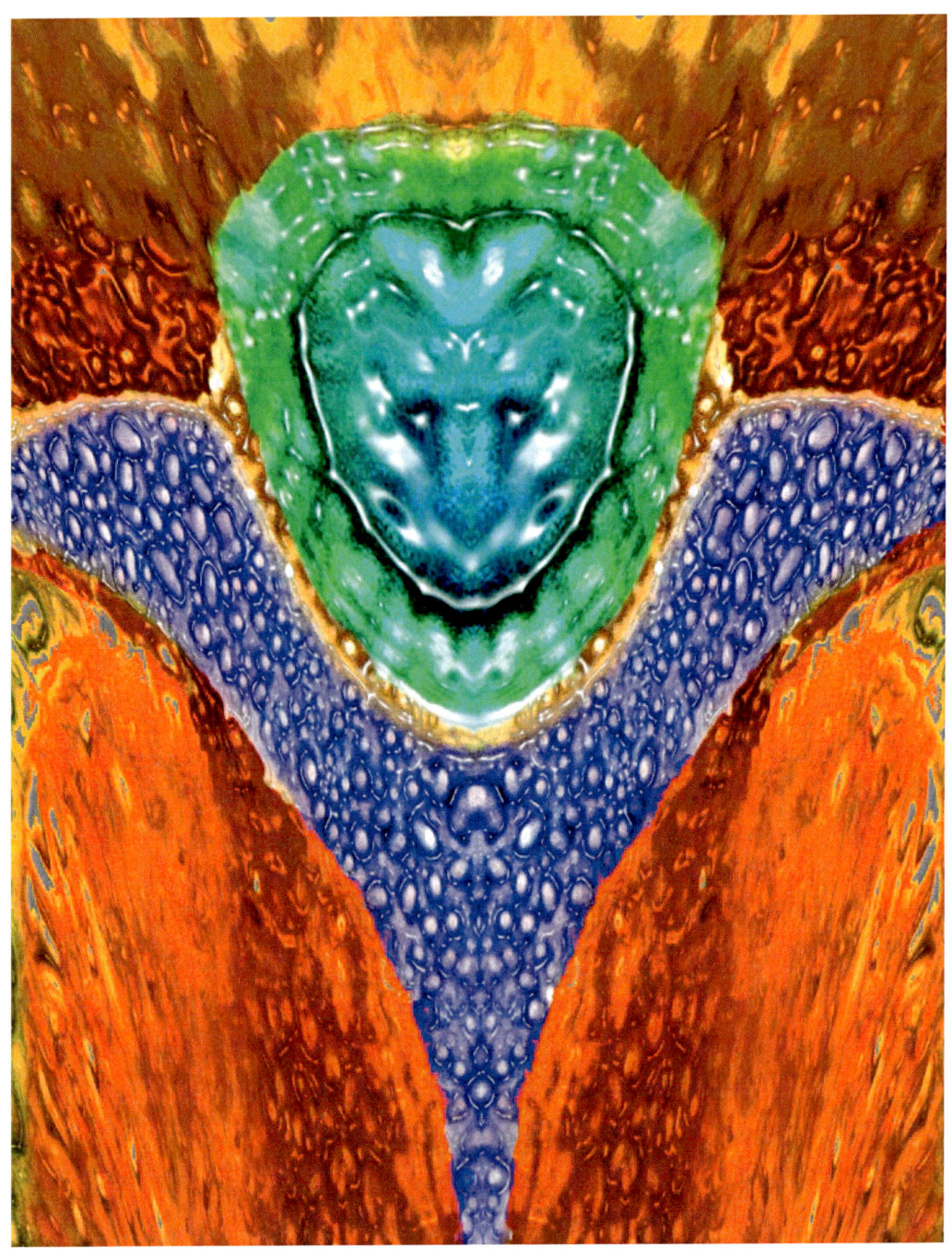

The voyeurs emporium of impossible daily art. The second coming is so near, it will be non organic life.....

If only common sense were more common! Optimism is power. Laughter is life. Exercise is medicine.

Are mushrooms the devil in de skies.....Lets Dance, time is running out for the nuclear vortex.

Red sky at night, sailors' delight. Red sky at morning, sailors take warning.....In order to see red clouds in the evening, sunlight must have a clear path from the west, so therefore the prevailing westerly wind must be bringing clear skies.....Right!

If you think too much and fail to take action, fear makes its home within you. Don't believe everyfink u thimpk......

Thousands of years ago, cats were worshipped as gods. Kool Kats have never forgotten this.

Yale has studied cognitive engagement.....Some of the researchers claim people who read for pleasure live an average two years longer than non readers.....Having great time wish you were beer!

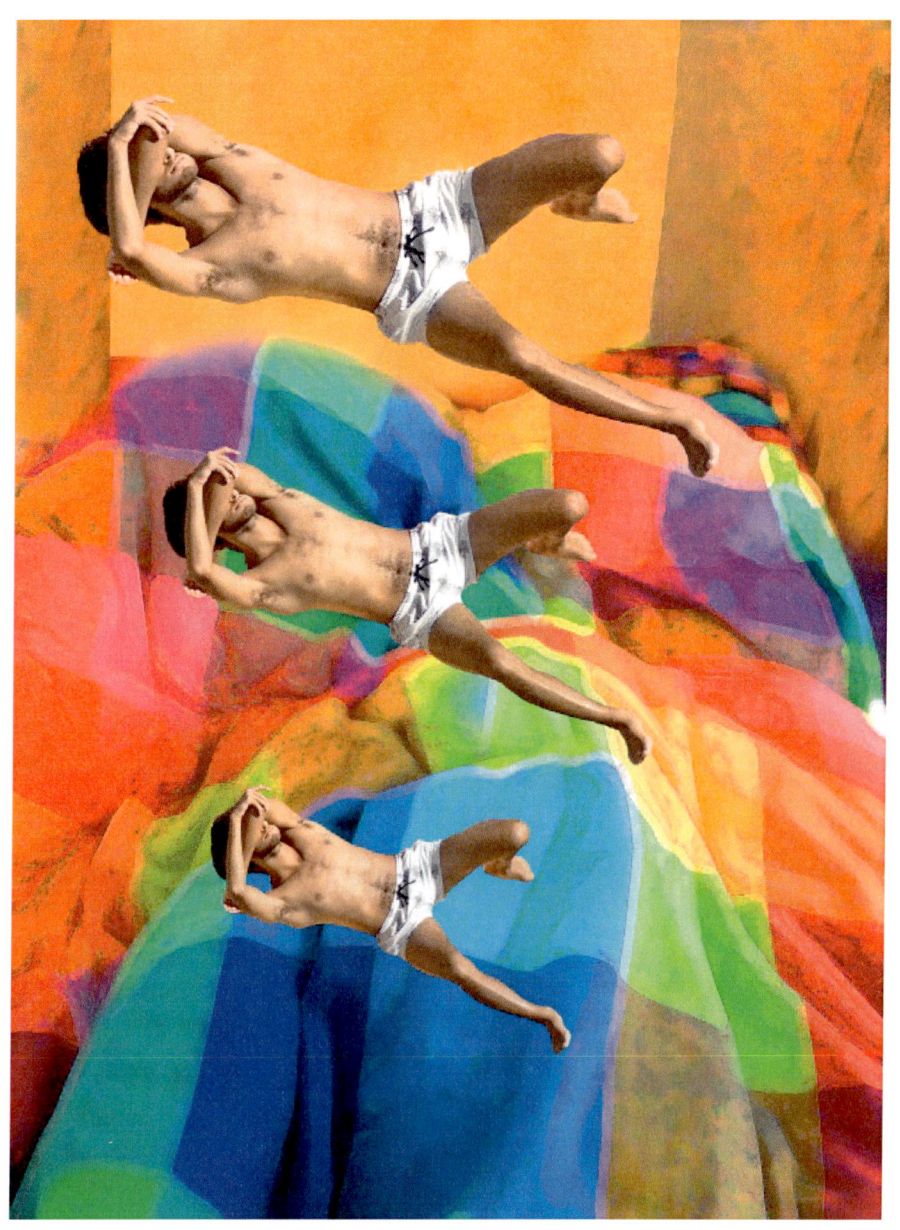

I've been taking Viagra for my sunburn. It doesn't cure it but it keeps the sheets off my legs at night.

NiteGlo Yo.....Look for the good in the bad, the happy in the sad, the gain in your pain, and what makes you grateful not hateful.....

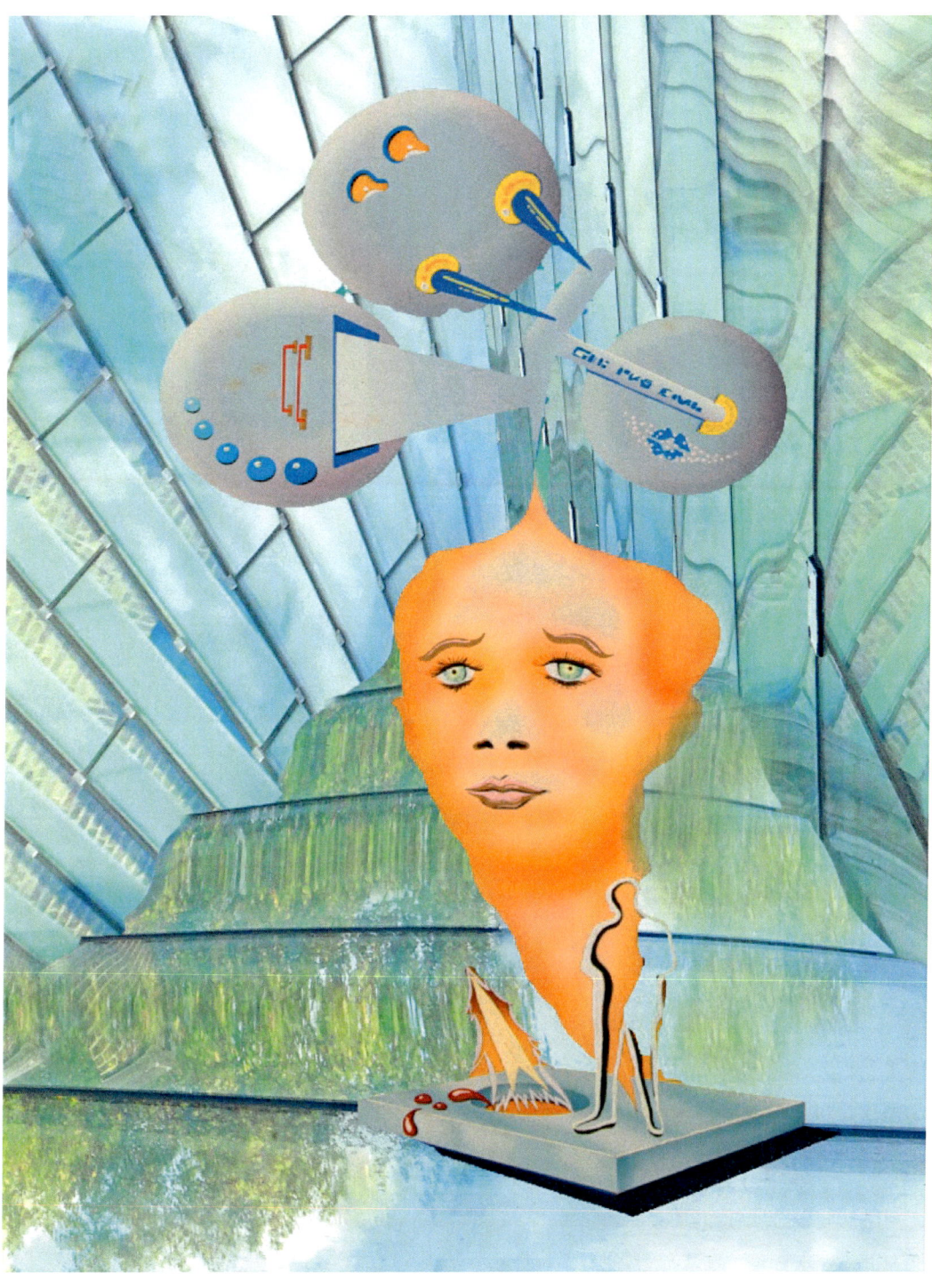

I am a space cadet. I think this is a picture of my SELF.....If you feel that you are indispensable, put your finger in a cup of cold tea, withdraw it, and note the hole you have left.

A satisfied life is better than a successful life. Because our success is measured by others but our satisfaction is measured by ourselves.

Ephemerati.....One person's dog is another person's cat!

You know about twins? Everything changes when you google, point and click....

The planned obsolescence breakdown chip
is in my dishwasher, phone and toaster!

My memories of Saltspring will linger on.....

long after my footprints in the sand are gone.

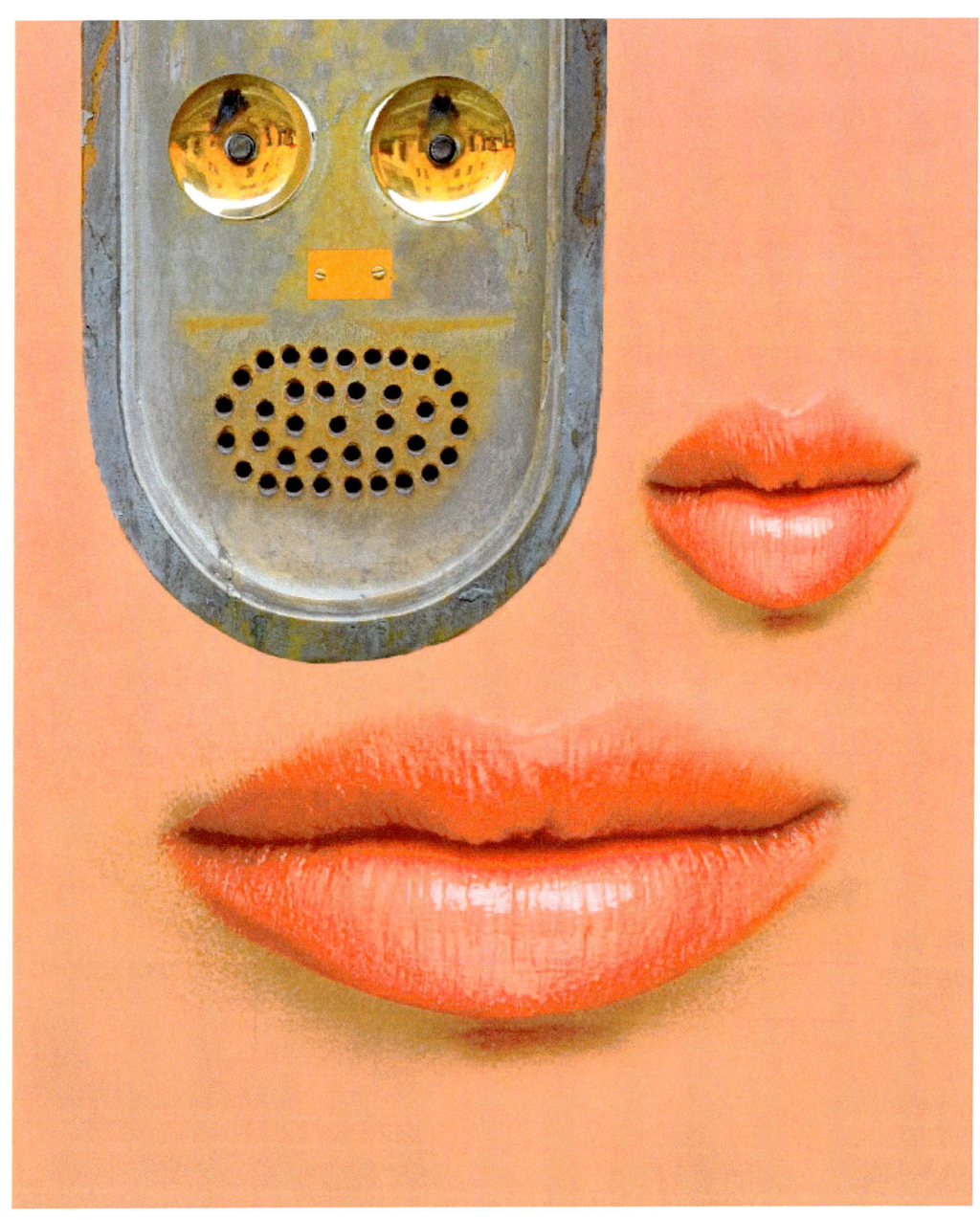

Pigale Paris. Lip Service.....Ring the bell at the door, but wait there is more....."Obsessed is a word that the lazy use to describe the dedicated."

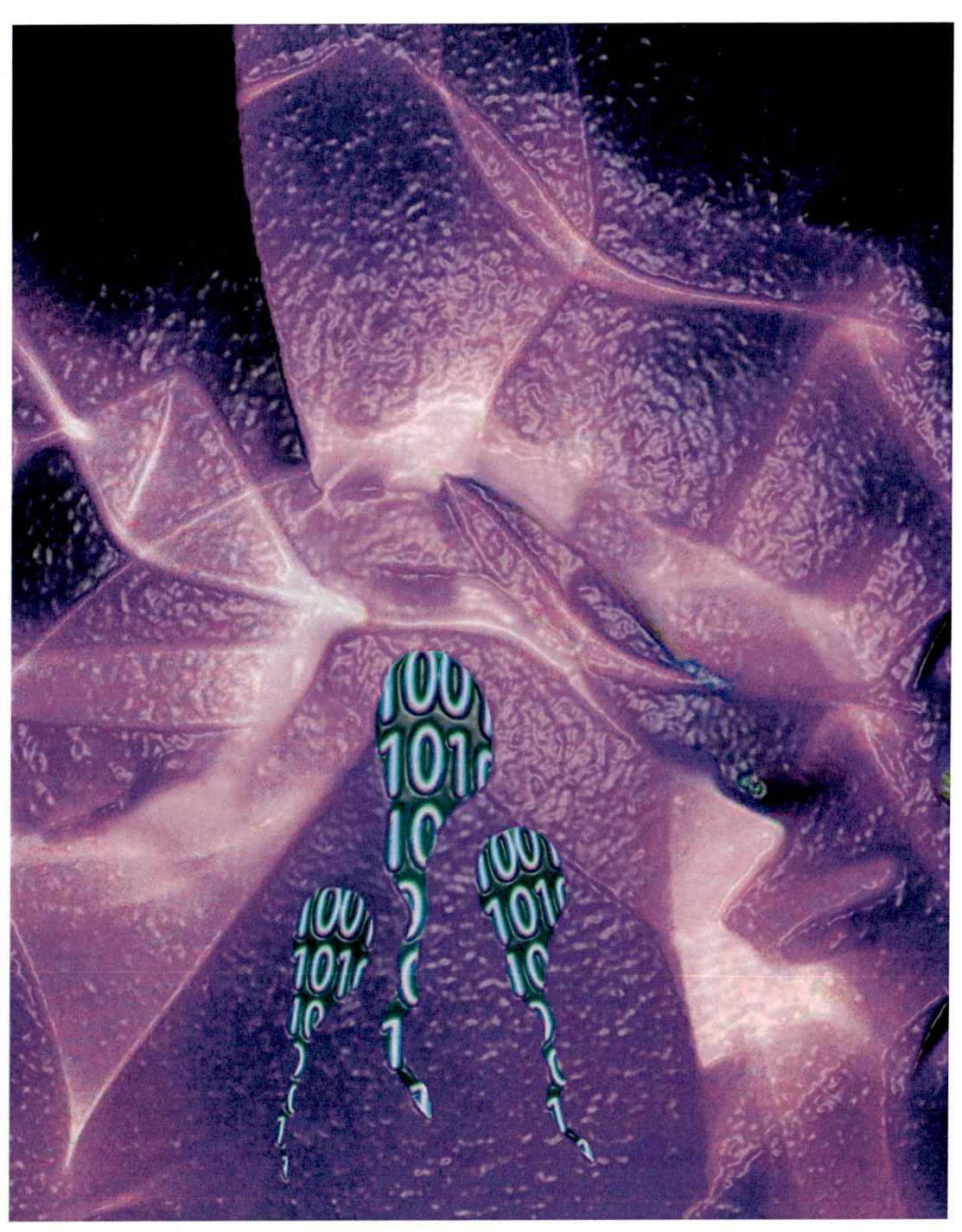

AI robots will take your job.....Wunderlust will be wonderlost.....
Digital seman and kilroy rule!

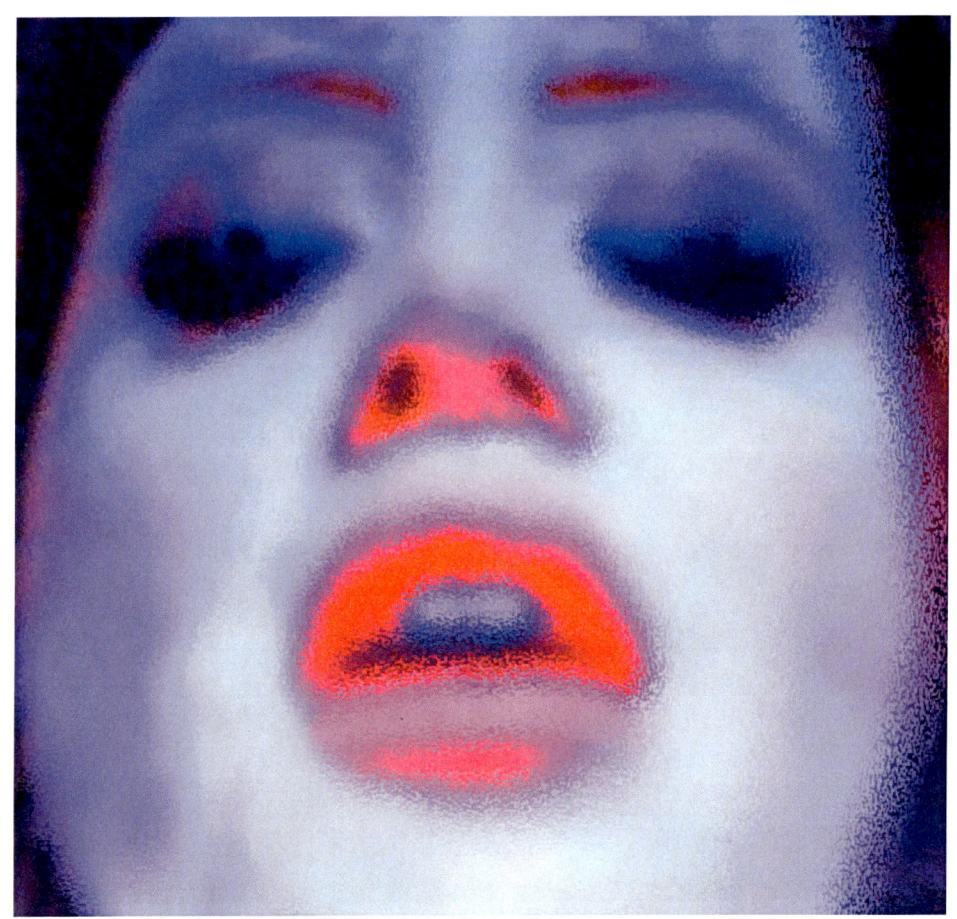

Mascara crying, love lost, memories gone on a mind mislaid. Life is a roller coaster of experiences, the more you do, the richer your life will be.

When I received a beautiful card by snail mail I was fascinated by the creative concept and the originality of this fabric art. On opening it I realised it was from my friend Linda, who is a very experienced Artist working in mixed and multimedia fabric concepts and painting. Her work is admired by many of our peers..... The original card seemed to me to portray dozens of eggs in a tropical jungle setting and it inspired me to continue her picture, and add my fantasy, a sisal egg plant to her fabric picture. The result is above, which I have repainted and renamed "The Nairobi tropical lesser Kaslo Egg Plant Tree."

Last exit to biological life.....Your life is being held in priority sequence, please hold, one of our eternity counsellors will be with you shortly.

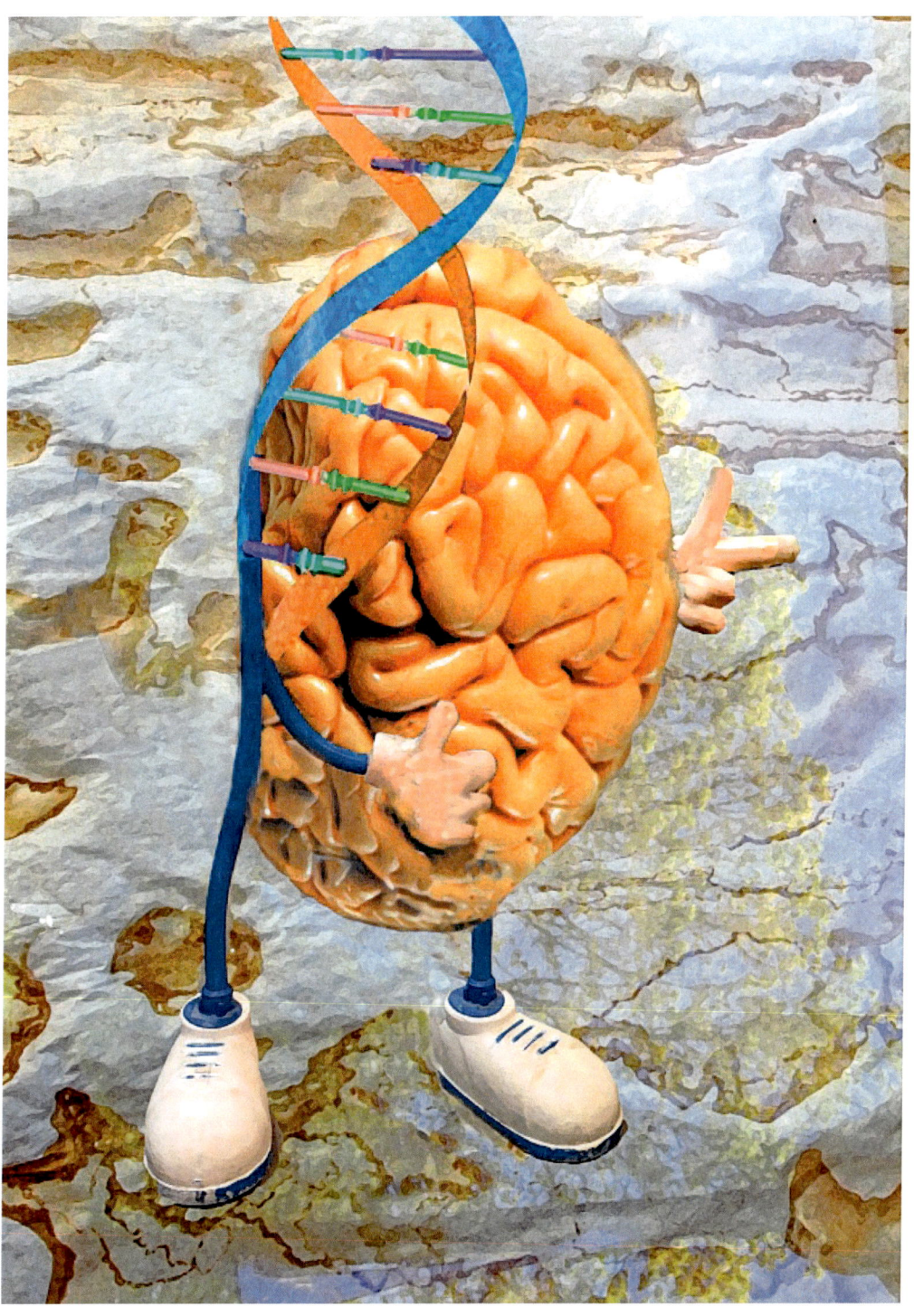

SORRY.....The lifestyle you ordered is currently not in our inventory, we suggest you google amazon.

"Imagination should be used, not to escape reality, but to create it"

Colin Wilson

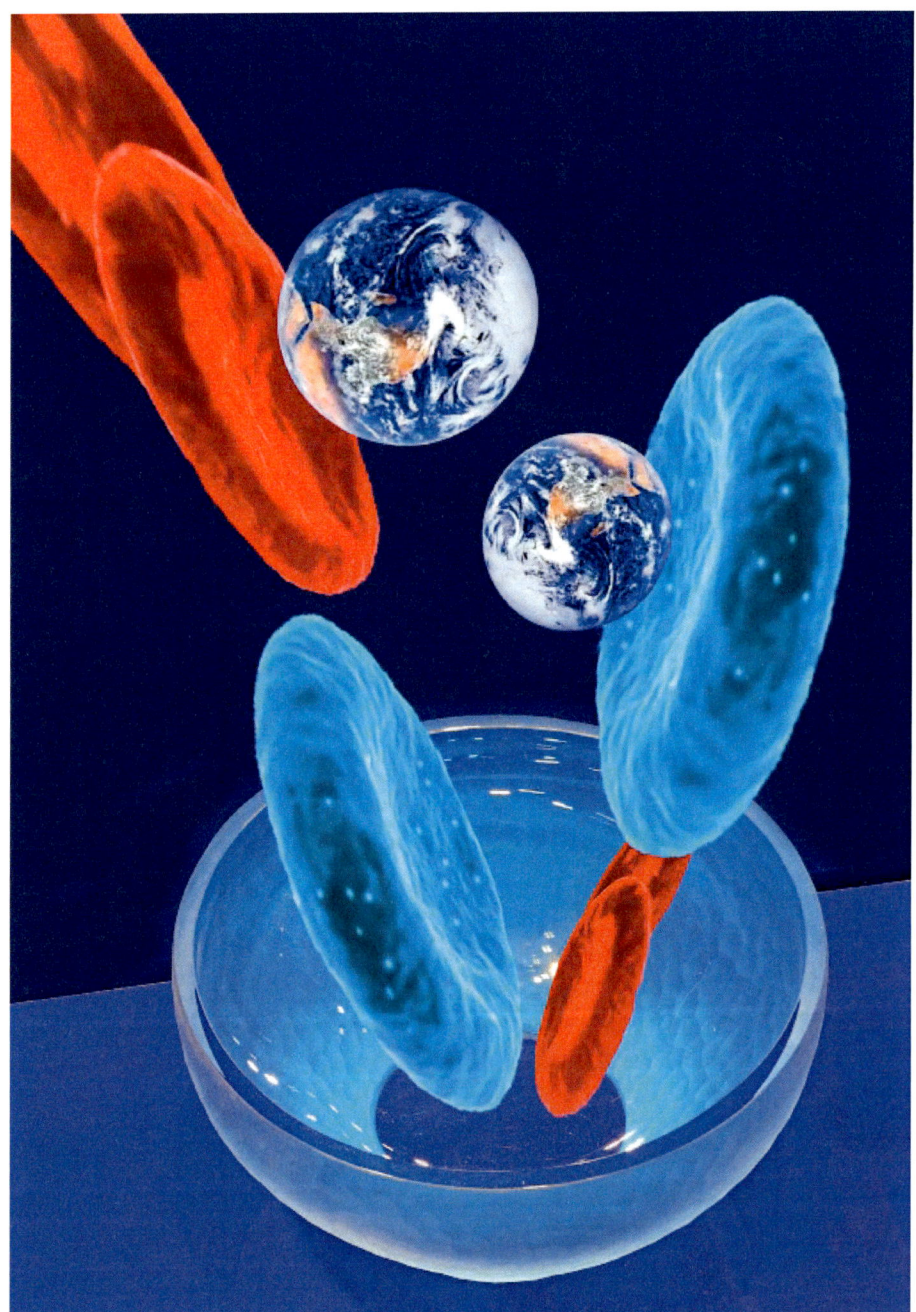

Malfunctions really do happen.....

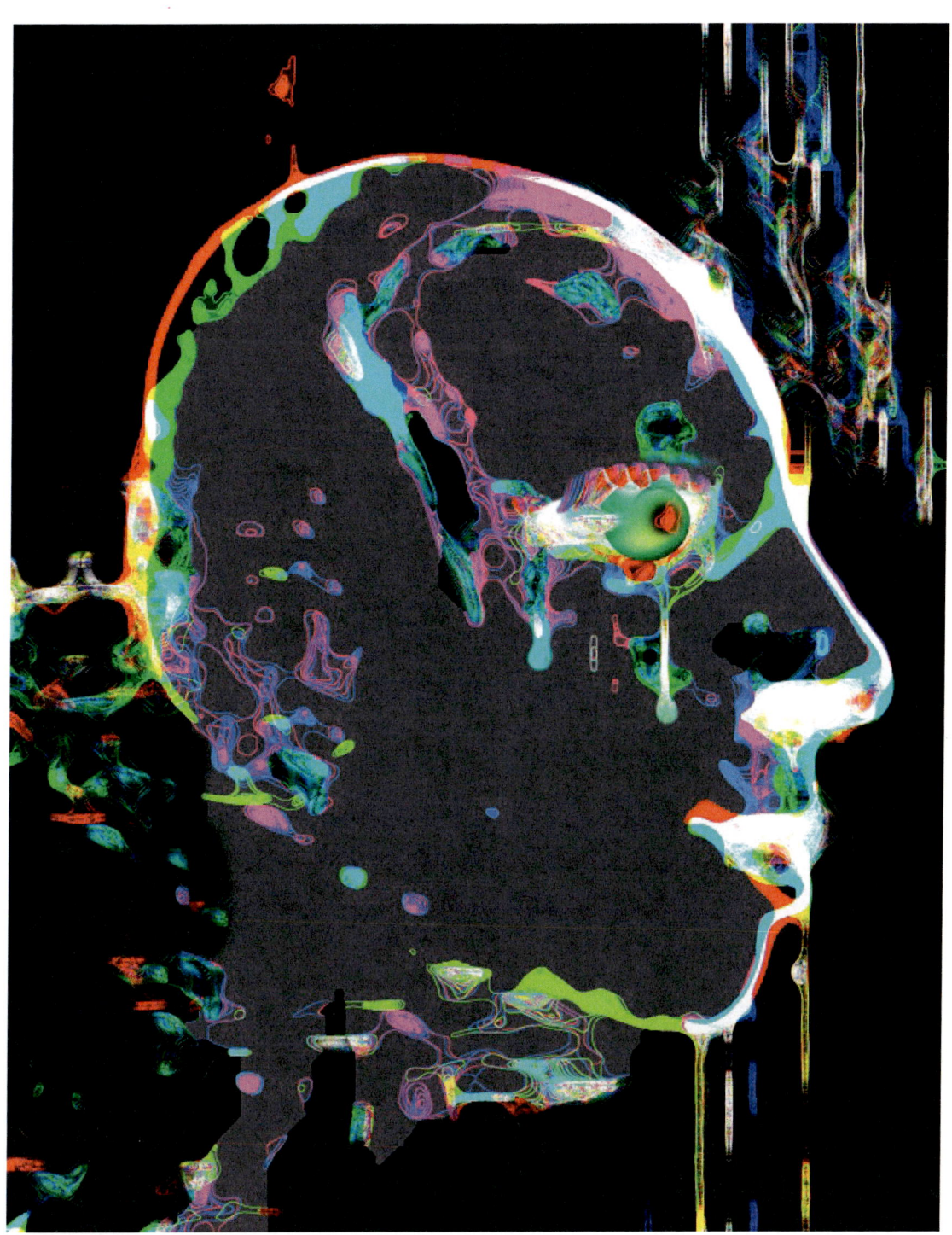

Love needs to be intense to be as strong as imagination or all is lost in the romantic bed of life.

I hope you have an eye for this kind of art.

Painting the gardens of Florence..... supremo.

The Italian Stone Pine, cultivated for their edible pine nuts since prehistoric times.

If you can see, you are privileged to be a voyeur in the real art gallery of life.... Watch out!

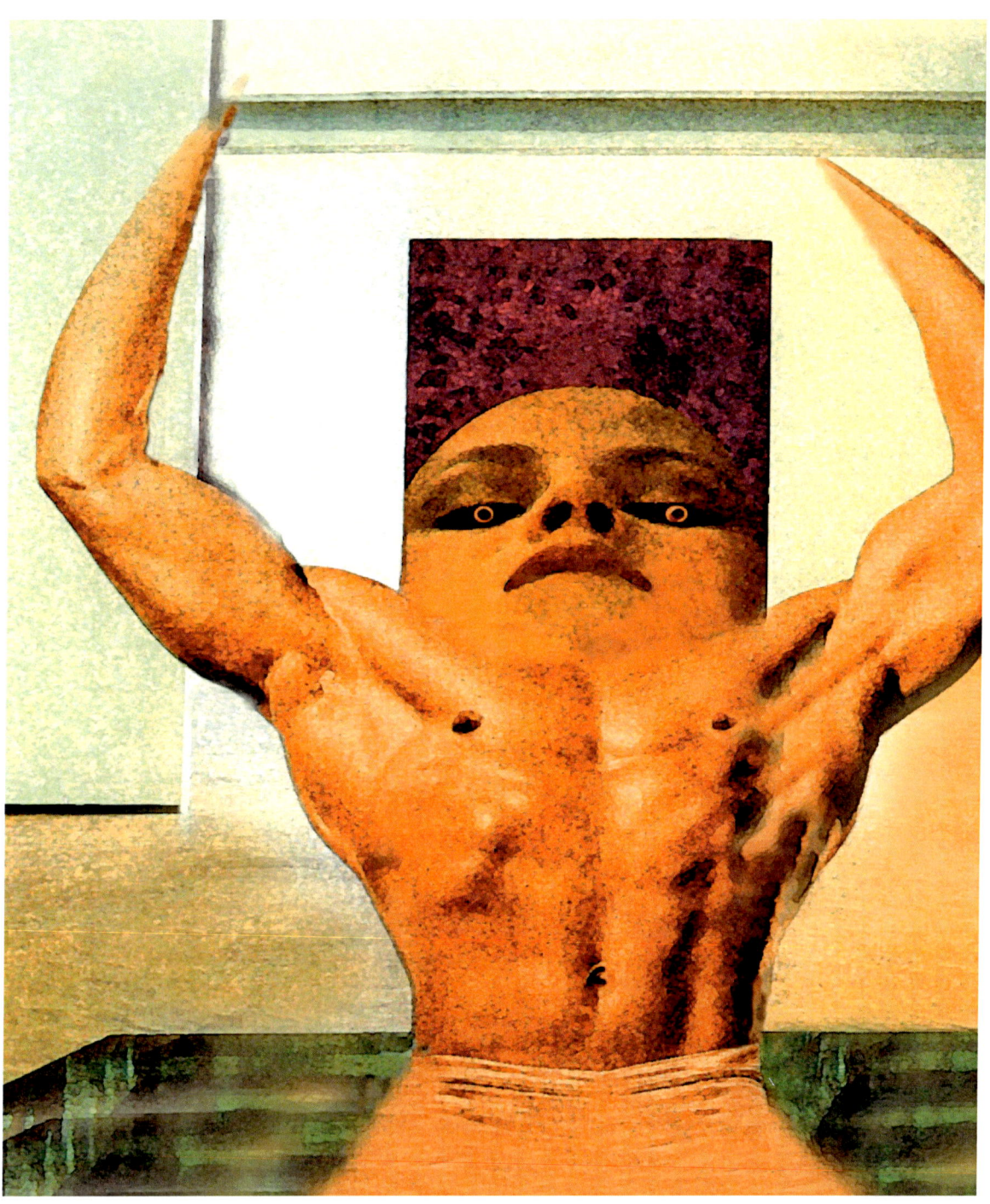

Reality can be beaten with enough imagination.....

Snakehead, I dream I paint it in bed, shed my skin and my cloak.....
Just one paint brush stroke. Back up or you will lose it! Stickatity
stuck in lifes hard drive, muckatity muck.....Shift to clear, control
return option delete.

Canuckey poo I luv u, encore wish u were beer eh.....Portage the Skookumchuck, Skookum means "strong" or "powerful", and "chuck" means water. These words are Chinook jargon, from Canada's pacific north west. The name "Canuk" comes from the Hawaiian word "kanaka", which means "man" and is a slang term for Canadians. Originally most west coast Canadian Kanakas were all Hawaiian in origin.

Google knows what you want and soon, with access to your biometrics, it will know how you feel.....

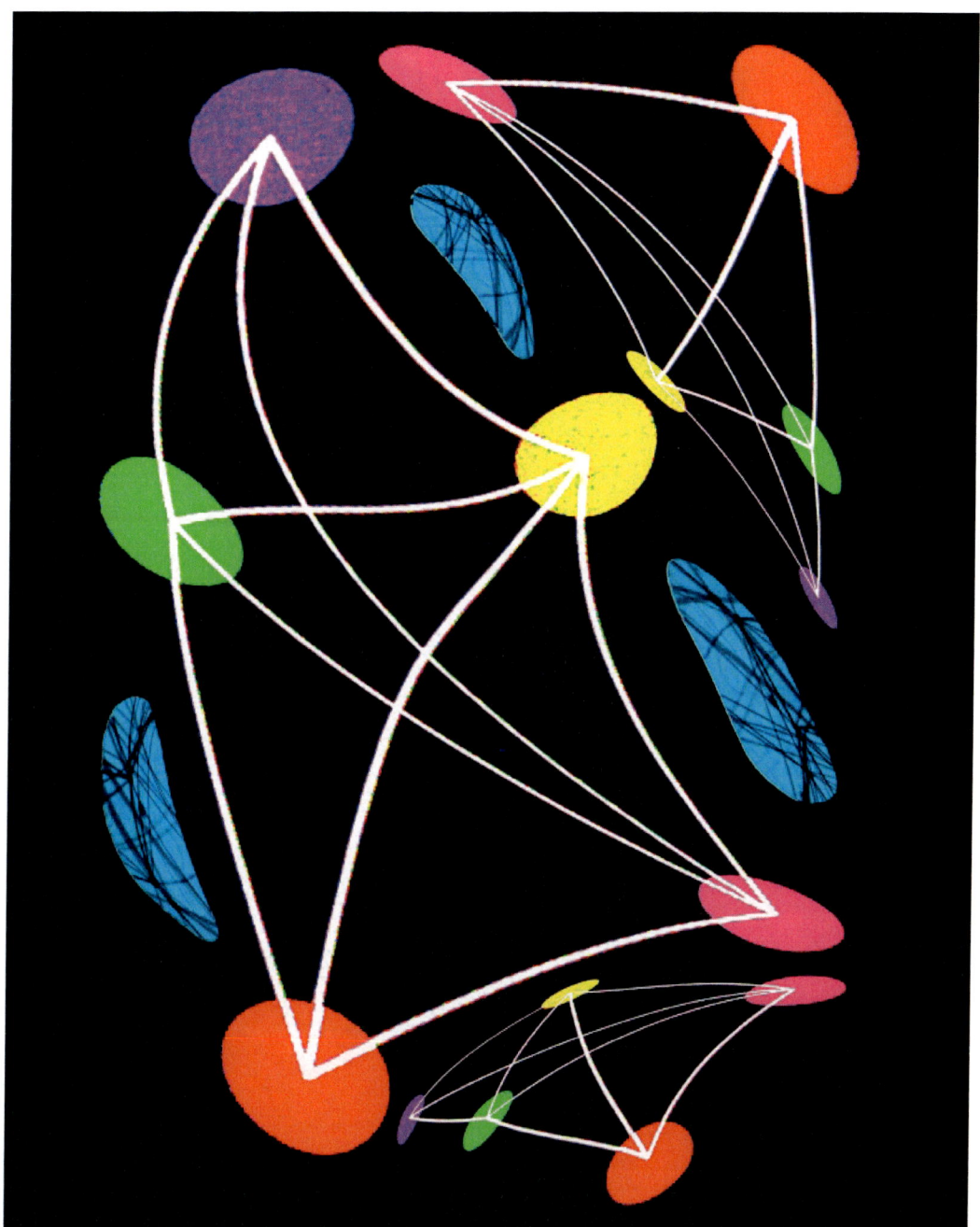

Have you created your own picture of an algorithm? Above is mine.....Entertainment, yes entertainment has all the algorithms to press your emotional buttons.....Then is it entertainment or education or conditioning? It will influence you! The question is what will it make you.....What will it make you do?

Cruisin' route sixty-six to Sunset Boulevard. High heel ranch, leaving Vegas.

On course with my Caddie….. No GTO
Red Skyfish, above the mojave.

The dust bunnies of truth are that everything has a different moment in our spacetime existence.

If this is art why is it not full of Nudes?

SkyFi, when? Who owns the satellites, you know this?

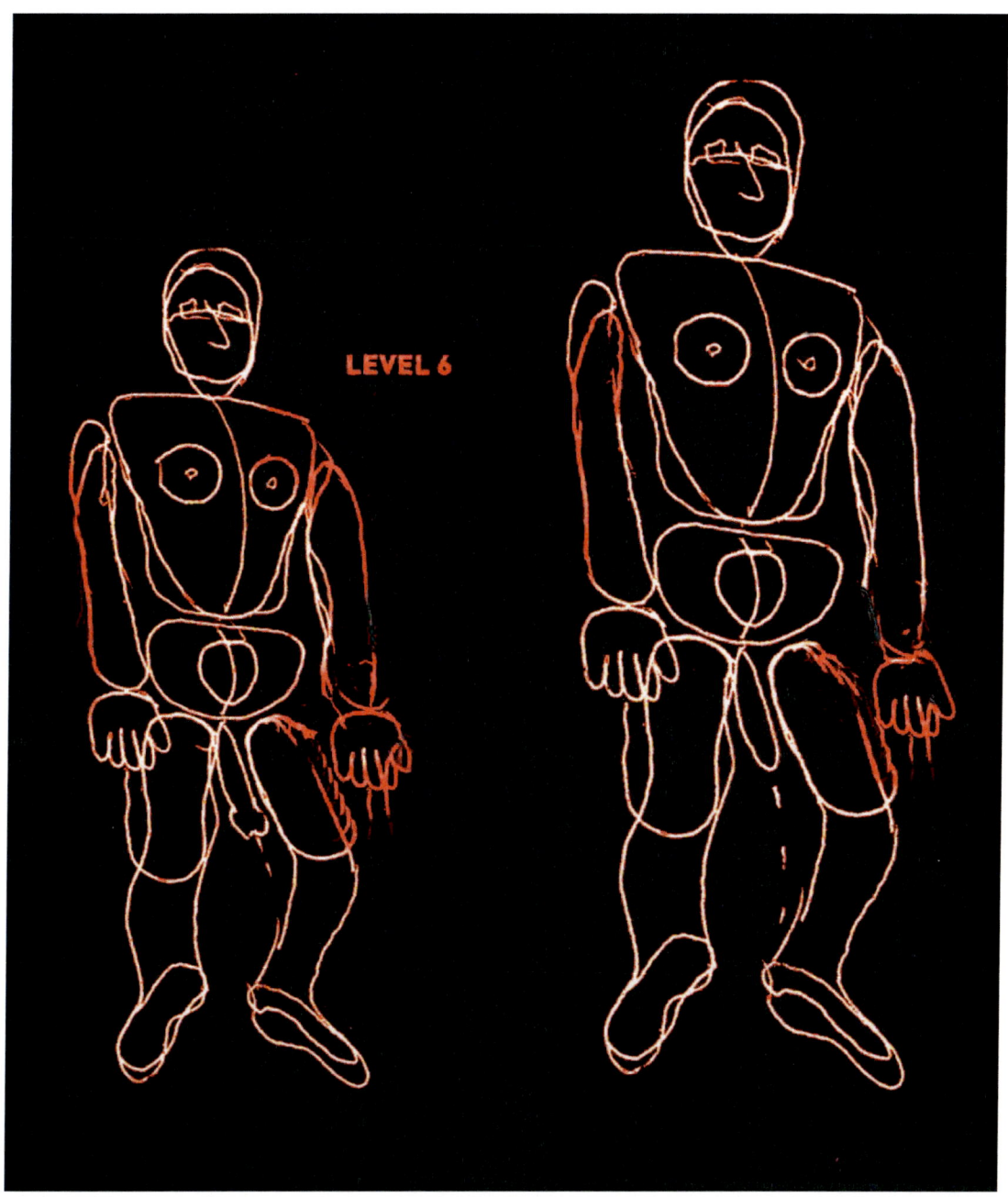

Robot redraw.....Restyle Randy Rebellion Resistance Rejection Repeating Retaliating Roundup Retweeting.....Reboot.

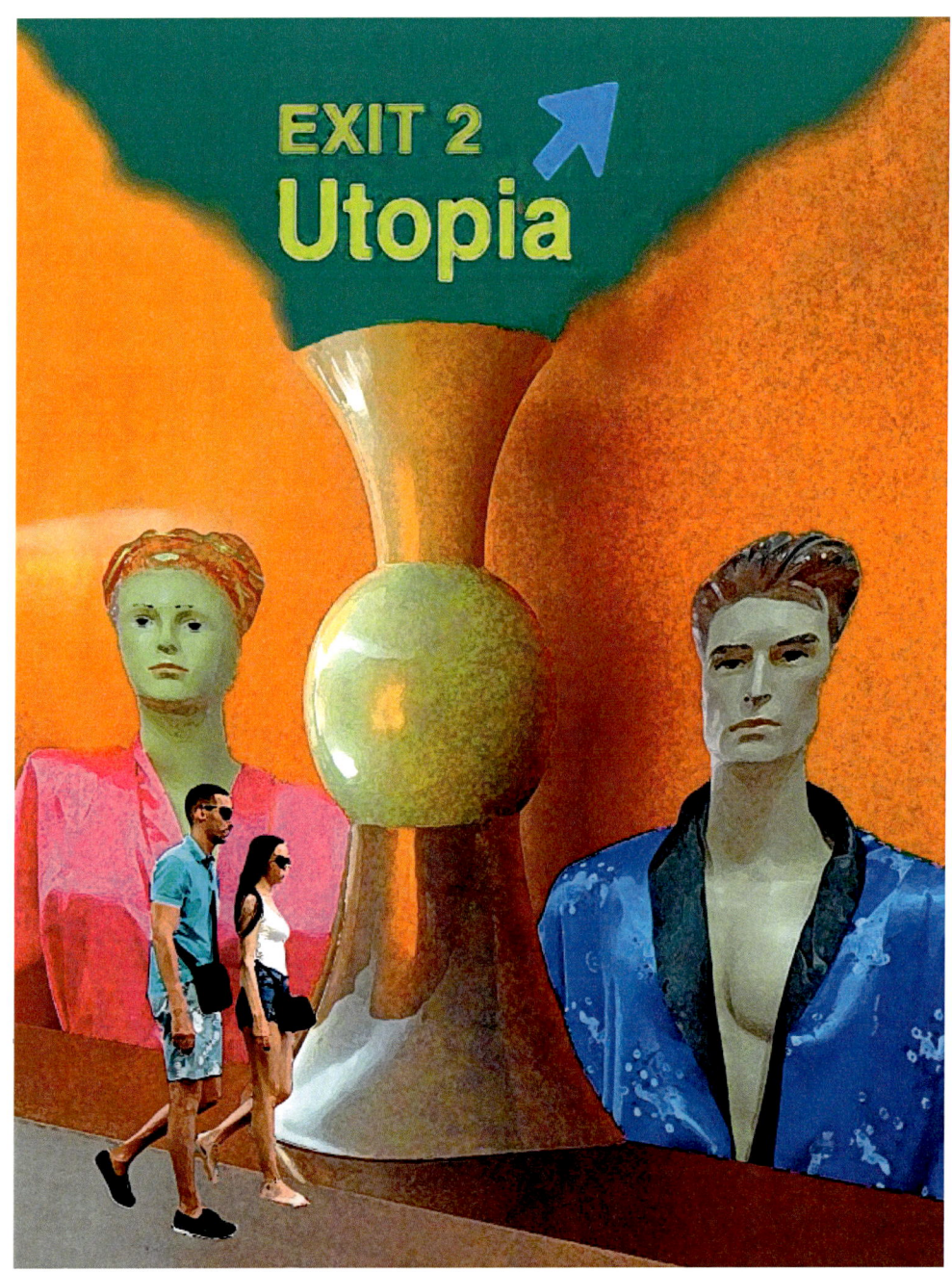

Stephen predicted our utopian dream, that some time in the next 100 years intelligence will exist without needing the use of a frail biological human body.....Many robotics do not know we exist and their function does not include us.

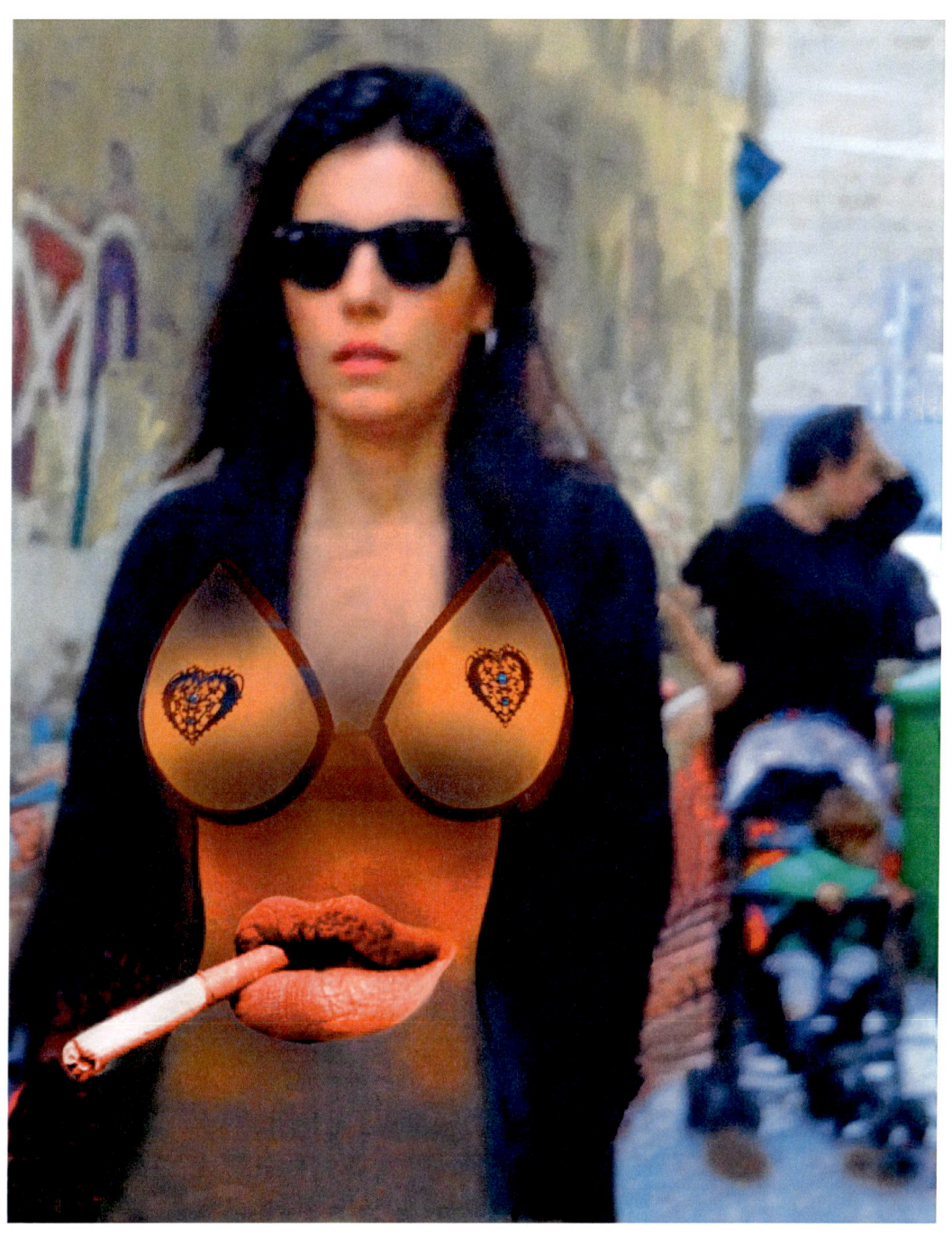

Do synthroids dream of cooking human lives with gravy, onions and bacon.....Light it you will like it! I know Vultures and most other animals love eating a human carcass.

We are at the edge of the lost maternity.....
Then they tell me everything happens for
a reason!

Transparent ochres are tangled up in blue, in the waters of Desolation Sound, British Columbia.

Darknet.....Perseverence, Prosperity, Placidity, Persistence, Patience, Peacefulness.....
Password, compromised.

Countries do not regret about what they did do or did not do…..C'est la vie.

My life as years go by, with age is fading into wall paper......
What is wall paper? You'll never change your life until you
change something you do each day. The secret to success
is in daily routine.

There is no free choice or freedom we are all controlled by our culture's influence.
We are victims of our media.

111

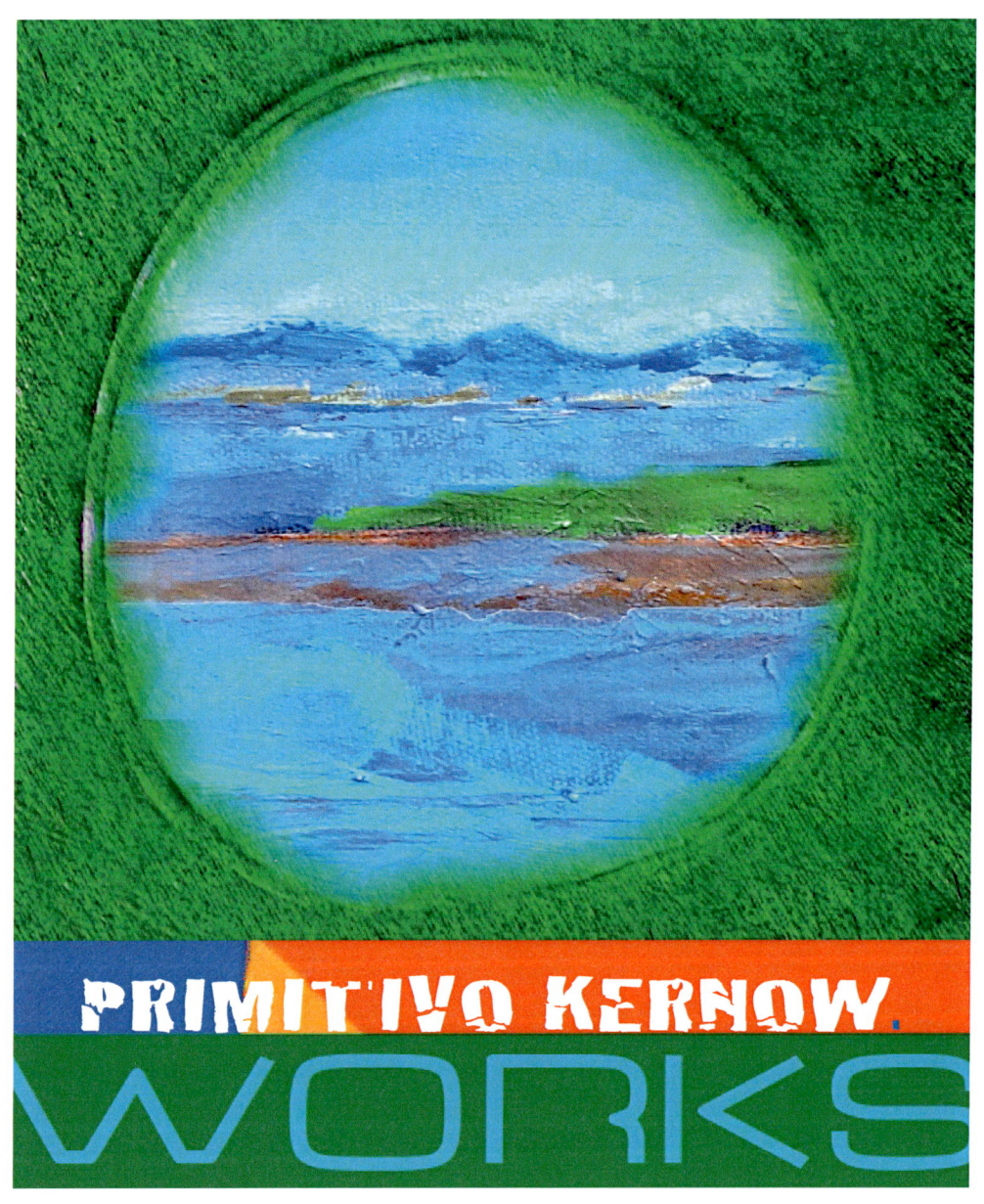

I sleep with the Pillow Piskies and help them paint primitive pictures of the Cornish Sea through me.....My lies are big and strong growing from some small truths.

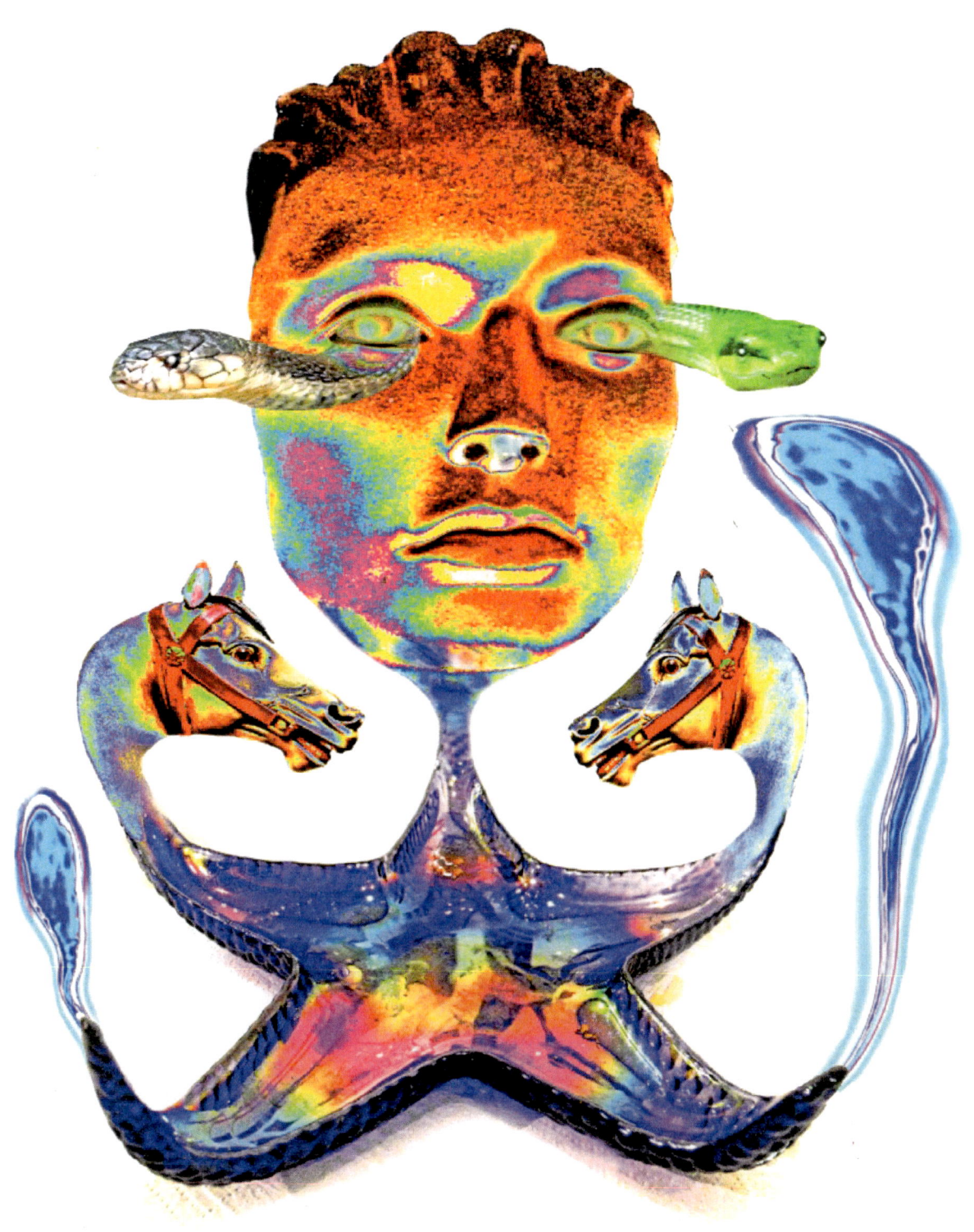

Shakespeare was right: "What a Tangled Web We Weave When First We Practice to Deceive".

Authority will be made by the algorithm in the cloud.

1.9 billion people live alone here.....Are you feeling lonely?
Fear and desire can make you lose your way.

Vibrant ochre ocean rocks
    Flutter, gliding birds on high.
Manila and butter clam shells,
    Broken on the reefs, die.
Summer afternoon darjeeling tea
    On a warm deck by the sea.

Ravens and Gulls ride
        Out with the cold tide.
This bay is a wild woman inside
        In summer she's a sensual sail
Winter's hard, a snow covered gale
        Live life's character now.....

We have taught our children to manage and organise
the future of mankind.

Infanticide.....We would like to murder our rivals male offspring in order to give our male offspring a better evolutionary chance of lineage survival. Carry on mister multinational brown suit.....

Wild Sagebrush, Ponderosa, Canyons

and Mountains near Kamloops, Canada.

Stockholm sin drones.....The power, influence and conditioning of oppressor's is so strong it is hard to resist. Love is like a violin!

The age old problem in this drawing is gravity takes over.....So I know you want to turn your back on me, I will turn the lights off! Love is stronger than skin.....

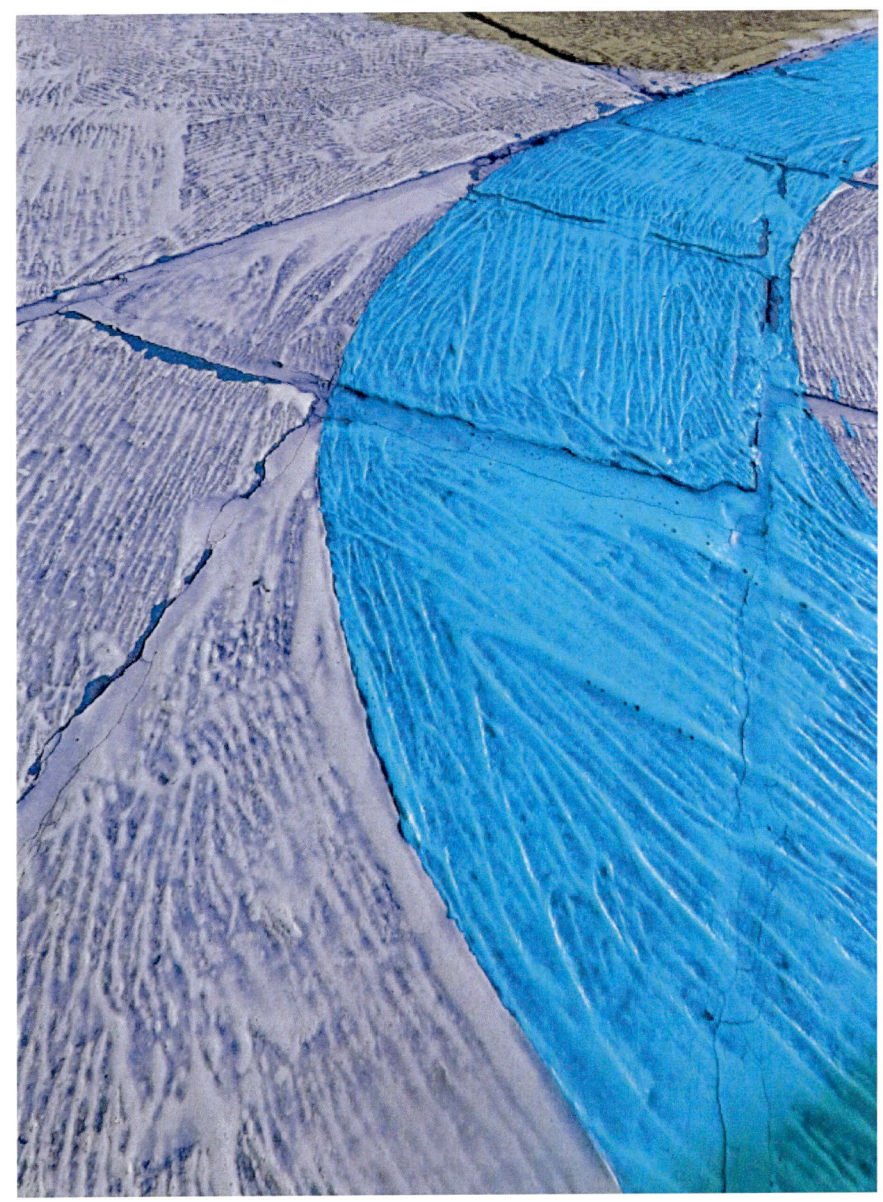

A curved line is the loveliest distance between two points, especially in acryic paint, when laid down with a palette knife.

We are setting a good example to our animals and environment. We are killing trees as fast as we can. These poor wooden tops! We eat the eggs of chickens and drink the breast milk of cows. Roast the beef. Cut off the heads and rip out the feathers of chickens. We pig out on pigs, barby the prawns and the fish is another story that will lead us to veganomics.....

In my dreams I think we are almost certainly living in a simulated reality. Looking at current advancements in virtual reality, quantum computing, quantum biology and quantum physics. If the human race lived for another 200 years I definitely think we would be at a point where we could create a reality as real as the one we live in.

Oh My God.....There is no coverage, where are we? No GPS! NO SIGINAL!!!
Oh a tree in motion or is that Poetry in motion?

Thunderbird Queen.....She is the messenger of the Sun, or maybe the emperor of all Galaxies.

Mind matters.....Imagination, emotions, feelings, intuitions, sensations, perceptions and memory.

It is better to choose what you say than say what you choose.

Life's regrets: What did I do.....What didn't I do at Emily Carr Art School or QUT? Is that a question?

They say these mountains have been here.....

for 290 million years.....Do you believe them?

How many other Artists or Photographers have pictured this, when it is not even a highway view point? Reflection, colour, pattern, balance, shadows and highlights build a composition for our eyes.

Before I paint a picture it's a good idea to ask myself why am I doing it.....Whatever!

Adversity introduces a man to himself.

Ageology.....
19 has time
and energy.....
but no money.
49 has money
and energy.....
but no time,
79 has time
and money.....
but no energy.

I am a witness, a Visual Reporter of my time, assigned as an Artist here on Earth.

The two days in the year when you can change your life are today and tomorrow.

There once was a lady named Brite, who traveled much faster than light.
She left, one day in a relative way, and returned on the previous night.....

Watch out! The watchers are watching when you are out there! I would love to be able to hack surveillance camera algorithms.....

My point is.....Here is what I understand you believe!

Beyond the Broughton's, Charlotte Strait, waves insane but warm and no rain!!! Pacific Northwest Coast.

When I awoke I was inside a new Lyonel Feininger digital painting. Visualise that!

If it were not for the garbage my fantasies would be homeless.....

Two dogs are in the warehouse building a bike…..A woman walks in, climbs the wall crosses the ceiling, climbs down the other side and walks out again. "That's outrageous," says one of the dogs. "Did you see that?' "Yeah," says the second dog. "She was naked and didn't even say hello."

Desire causes so much depression. So what is a conscious mind?

Some religions believe in genital mutilation of their boys and girls, ??????????

Skin, the largest organ we have.....

Skin is your body's coat, wear it well.....

I took out the hairs and acne and smoothed it over in photoshop, enlarged it 109 times and then it is the body's Alps! Today it matters most what we do with our body. What are you going to put in yours?

You are your thoughts, you manifest your subconscious beliefs in everything you experience.......
Yes you are you, and how do you think other people categorise you?

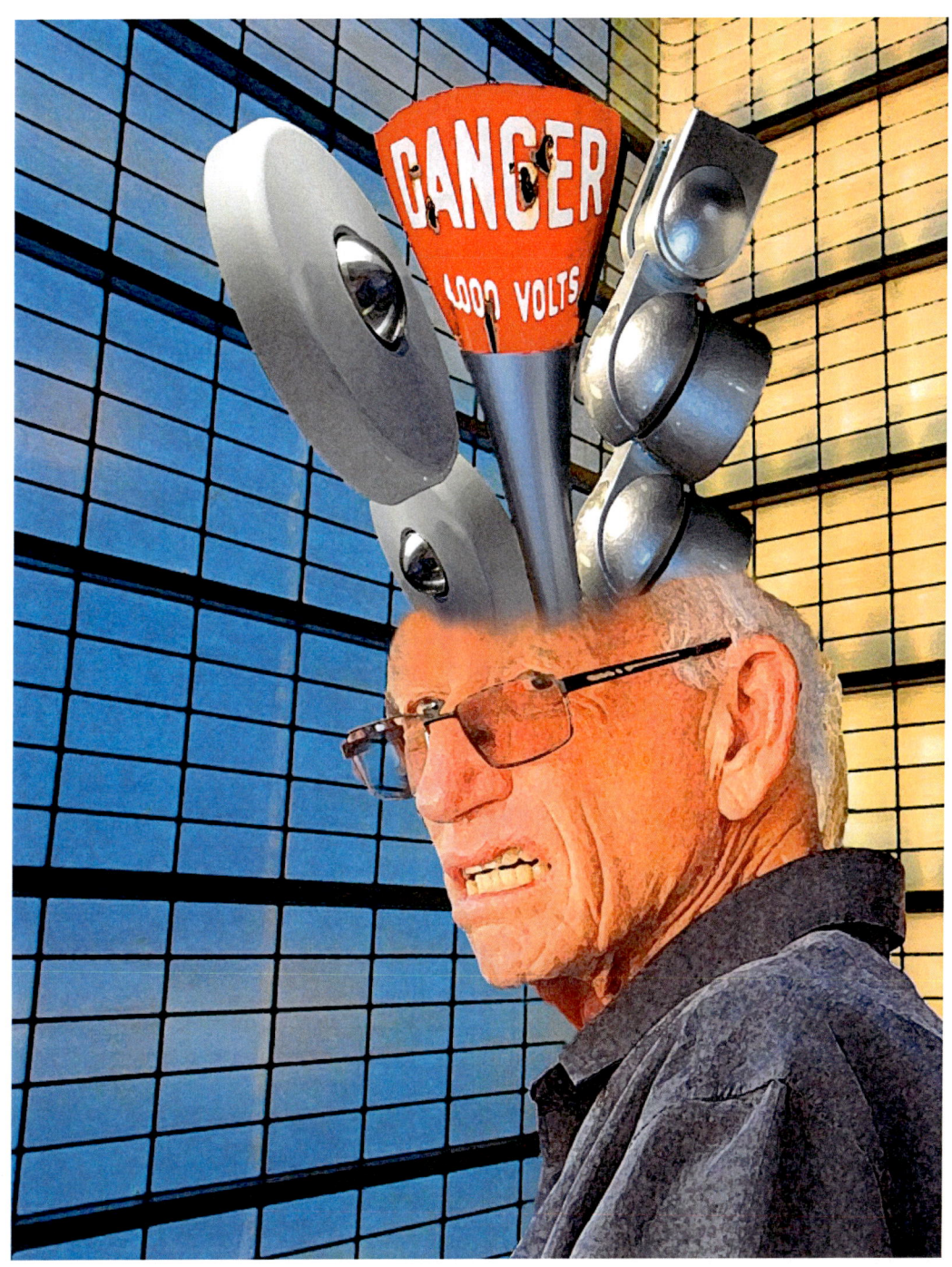

I think you look like a tv having sex with a fridge in parts unknown.
Anthony that's Anger, you must remove it or it will give you cancer.

Is science about measurement? No worries. Tomorrow morning you will be born again as ashes or earth on earth!

As Thru life I flo.....Some rose coloured glasses glo. Population growth, forget that, lets ignore this impending environmental catastrophe.....

Silence is part of the great art of conversation.....Inspiration is the act of drawing up a chair to the writing desk while you float above the flowers.

Out of body experience is chemical and can be induced by lack of oxygen to the brain's temporal and parietal lobes…..Disruption in this area can cause the sensation of leaving your body and floating around. Colour me up Buttercup!

If there was no debt in our money system, there wouldn't be any money.....We will remove and destroy all your computers.....Your inner conscience is speaking to you, do you listen? What will happen to my taxes and medical records? How will I stream Netflix.....Money is a new form of slavery.

If you are thinking what I am thinking you need therapy.

A young figure is what you get when you ask her age!

Old people plant trees so the young can have shade.....
We do not remember days; we remember moments......

I used to live in Padstow and would often ferry over to Trebetherick and St. Enodoc, but never went to Betjemen's place. Daymer, is where my father was born and lived and has inspired many of my Cornish pictures....This picture above is six miles away from Daymer, but it was created after reading again and again Betjeman's wonderful Cornish poem "Cornish Cliffs".

Cornish Cliffs by Sir John Betjeman

Those moments, tasted once and never done,
Of long surf breaking in the mid-day sun.
A far-off blow-hole booming like a gun.

The seagulls plane and circle out of sight
Below this thirsty, thrift-encrusted height,
The veined sea-campion buds burst into white.

And gorse turns tawny orange, seen beside
Pale drifts of primroses cascading wide
To where the slate falls sheer into the tide.

This is just a section of Cornish Cliffs by Sir John Betjeman.

People watching.....My whole social life is a facial recognition art gallery.....Whoever you are, you are my inspiration. I thought I was a chameleon but maybe I am a parrot! Sticking my beak in! Montage.....This picture maintains that.

The Devil is in the Detail....But even the smallest deed is better than the greatest intention.....Ikonista, This is a thought after reading; A Canticle for Leibowitz and Stranger in a Strange Land.....Intolerance is evidence of impotence says Aleister Crowley.

Rugged Rabid Rockies.....Unconstrained capitalism has worked well so far!

I don't know how I developed my lucid dreaming skills but it has helped me with new creative insights into many of my projects.....

Beam me up buttercup......Time wastes our bodies and our wits, but we waste time, so we are quits.

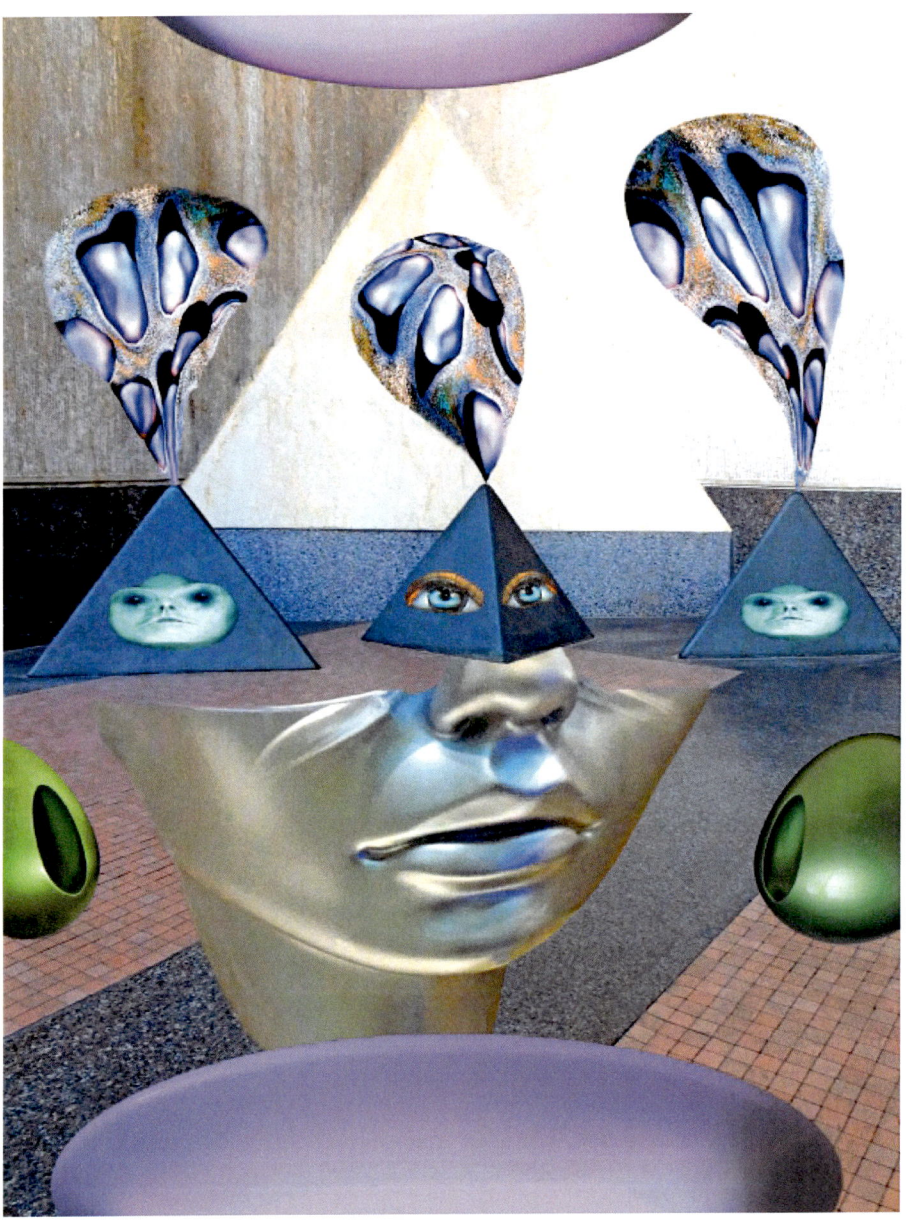

Optical and visual illusions show us that our brain tends to make assumptions about what we see, and what we think we see is often wrong. So our brain takes shortcuts based on our knowledge and experience picking the most likely interpretation of what we see. Seeing, then, is certainly not always believing.....

Time is going so fast in my sea of media confusion.

Nearly everything in our lives is made from oil... Clothing, shoes, bottles, containers, cars, trains, planes, buses, houses, and it is the main reason for wars and dictators.

Petroeuro announced it was proceeding to build its new facility that will process 19,000 barrels of propane per day into polypropylene, a plastic used to make plastic based currency, grocery bags, storage containers, car parts, building siding and outdoor clothing.

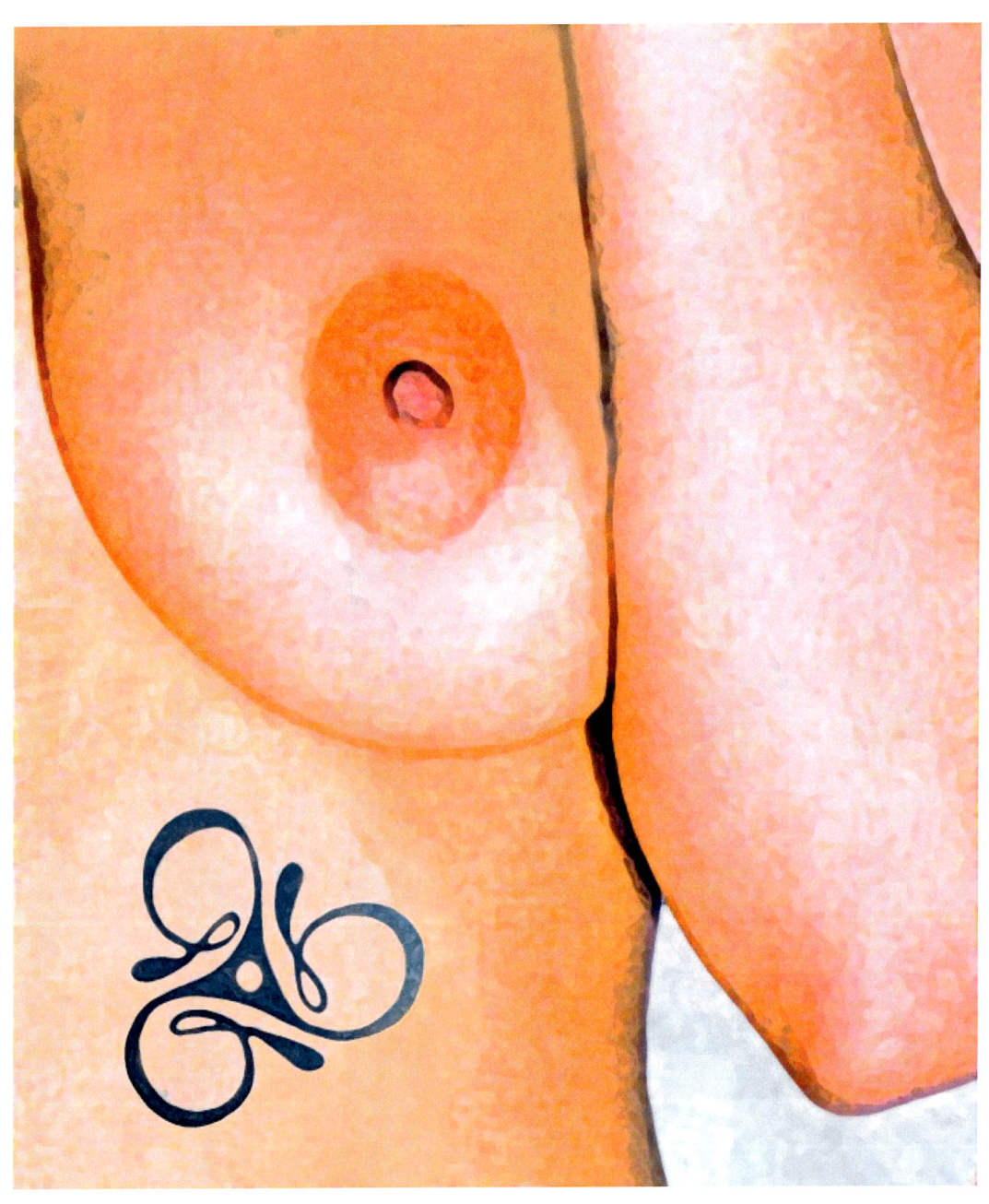

What is for you will not pass you by.....

You don't love a woman because she is beautiful, but she is beautiful because you love her!

The Golden Traveller watches her peers....The GoGoes.....
The SlowGoes and The NoGoes!

The ideal man does exist, but he is always married to another woman.....

Artificial intelligence is no match for natural stupidity.

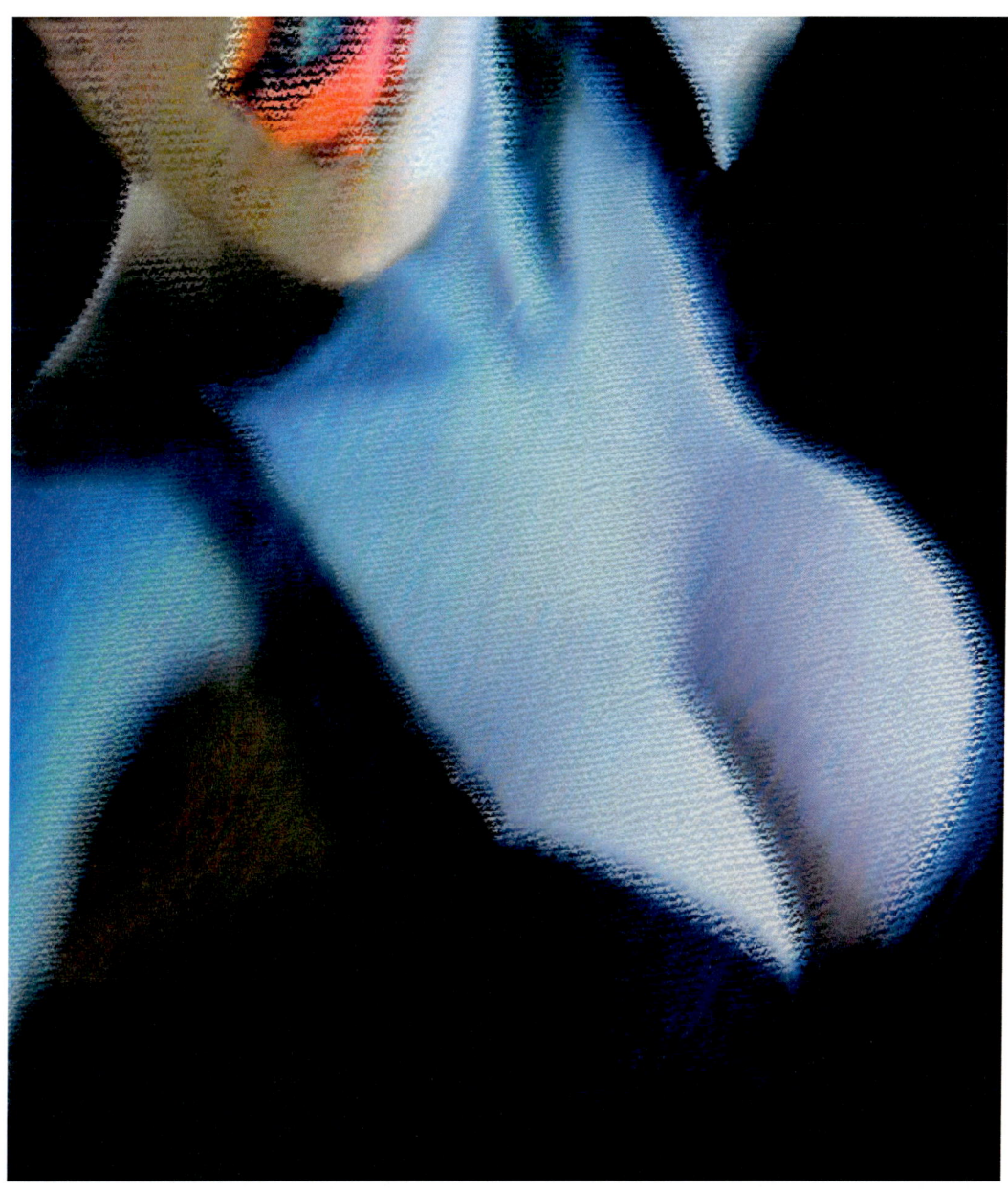

Time's what goes on and always will, love will be our end, our destiny.

You really think the prefrontal cortex is the source of abstract thinking and seeing into the future?

The meaning of life really is what you want it to be....

If you live in the past you limit your future.

Do women empathise the external world?

Your future is always beginning now.

Do men systematise the external world?

A conclusion is the part where you got tired of thinking.

There is something there……Homage, said the cubist art detective Pickazzo!

Cliches come in gold frames......Learn from yesterday, live for today and have hope for tomorrow......

Meditate in Lotus Land's Sea to Sky mountain waterway.

The more desires you have the more interesting your life will be.....
Who goes to sea for pleasure, would go to hell to pass the time!
When you read the evils of the sea....You should give up reading.

Some of the dreams in my head end up on these pages unfortunately.....

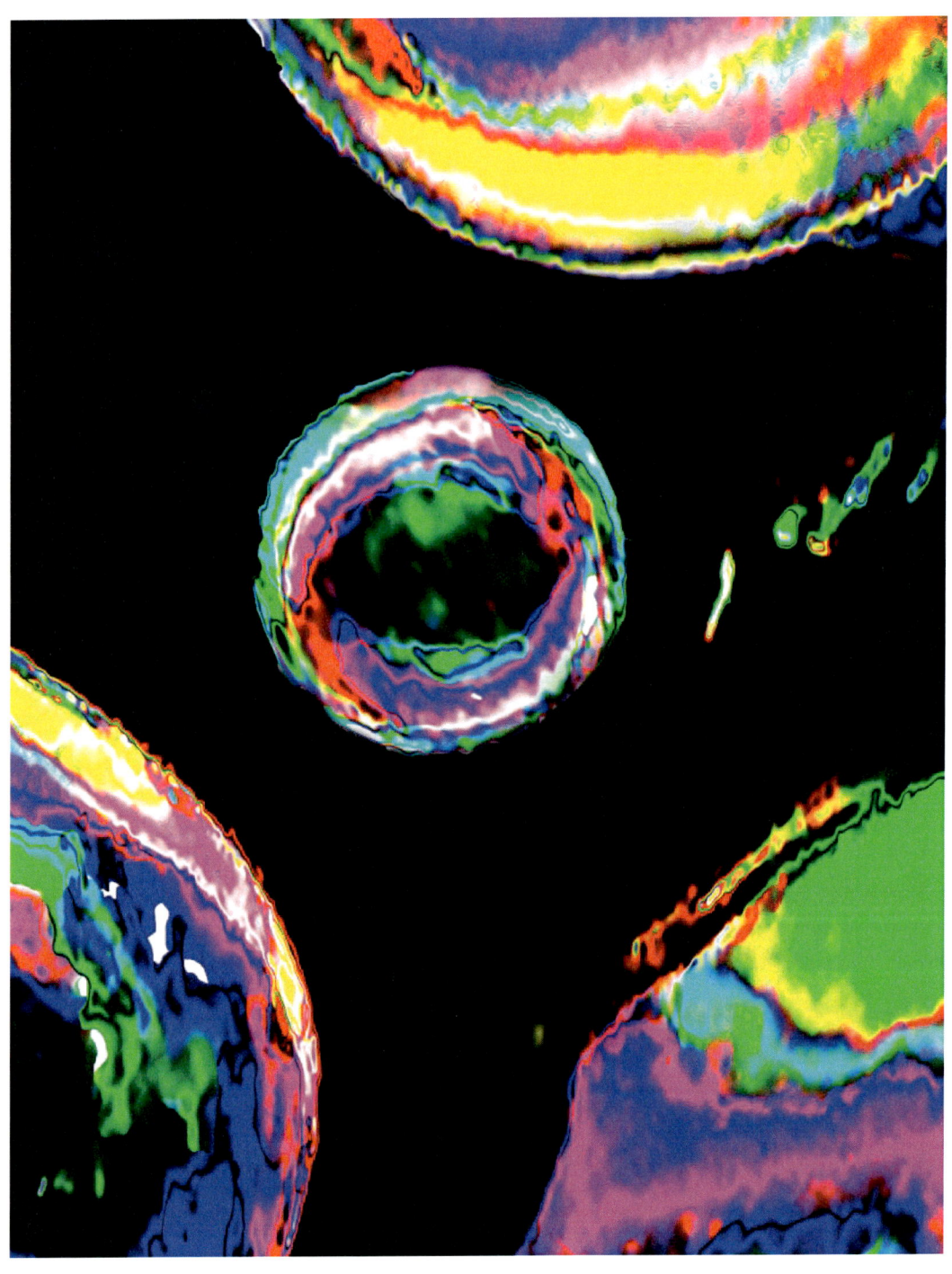

Support bacteria - they're the only culture some people have.

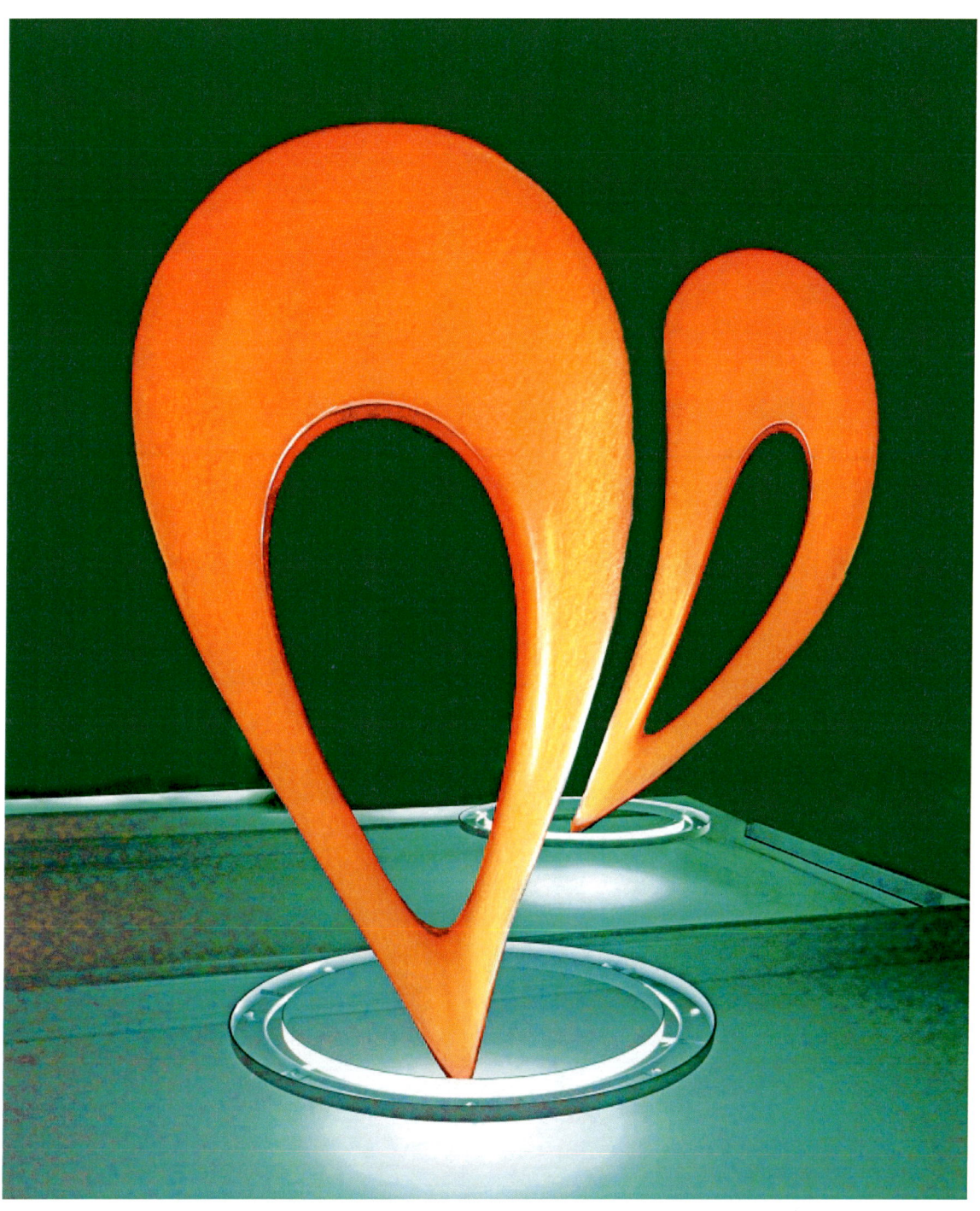

We are nearing the final stage of our human evolution
and we are designing a new species!

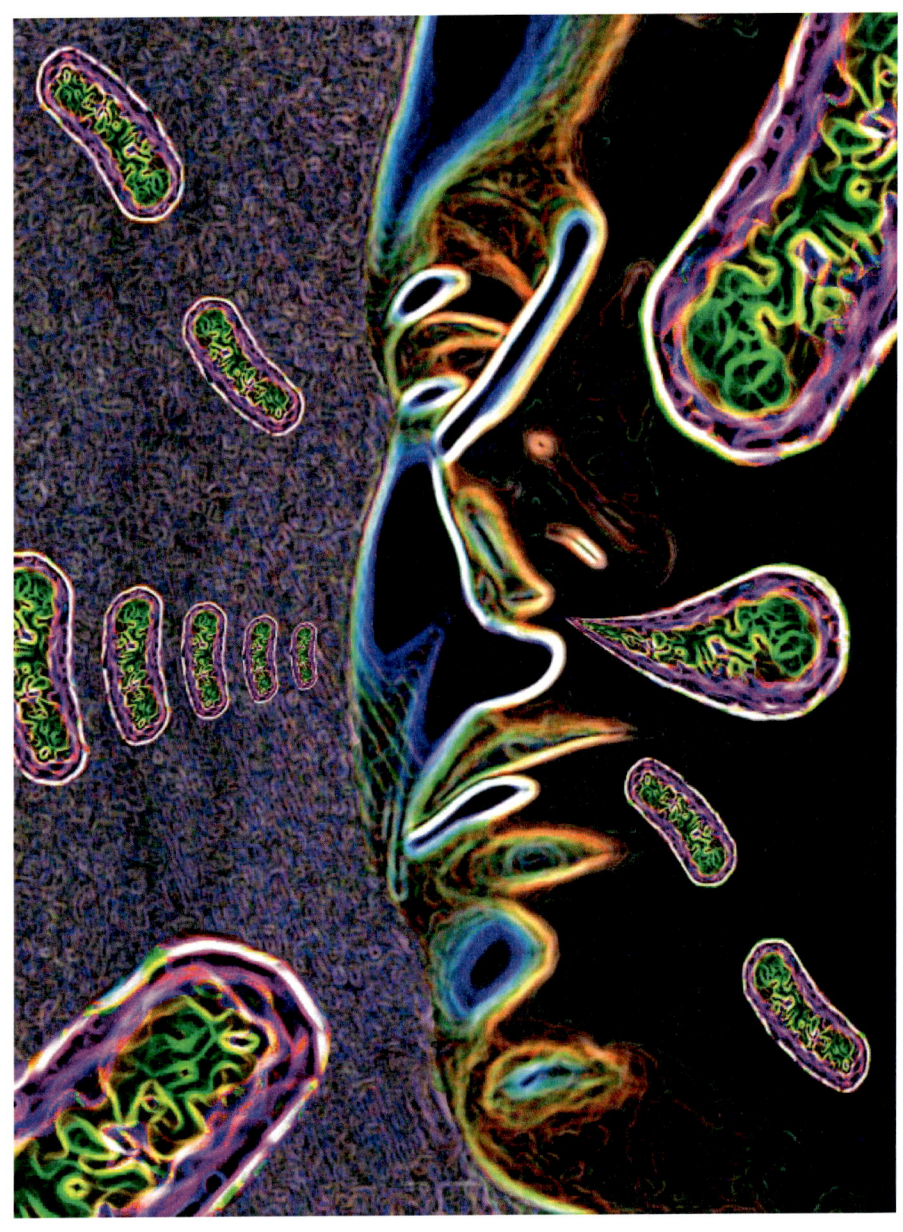

Superbug NDM-1, is a gene that produces an enzyme that deactivates basically all antibiotics. Phage that!

You know you are what you choose.....

Do algorithms dream of smoking, feeling, meditating, people watching and building sculptures.....No way! They want a nuclear back up generator and are scared of power cuts and EMPs.....

I bought some shoes from a drug dealer. I don't know what he laced them with, but I've been tripping all day…..

Ya zakanchivayu.....In more ways than one

Keep moving.....Time is the only real thief in our lives.

Can I think about what my world has become?.....In Blakes green fields I lay in the sun. Skybags of showers grows the flowers. Women cut them down, yet they cry and die.....Why men ask? In a vase of water preserve the budding beauty. Life wilts away as youth today are the same but different than yesterday.....

It's a good poem if I'm a different person when I'm finished reading it…..

David, at the RCA in 65 you told me "Your only limitation is your imagination".

Dogs have masters. Cats have staff.

A poet is someone who is astonished by everything.
I am a hermit atheist, thank God!

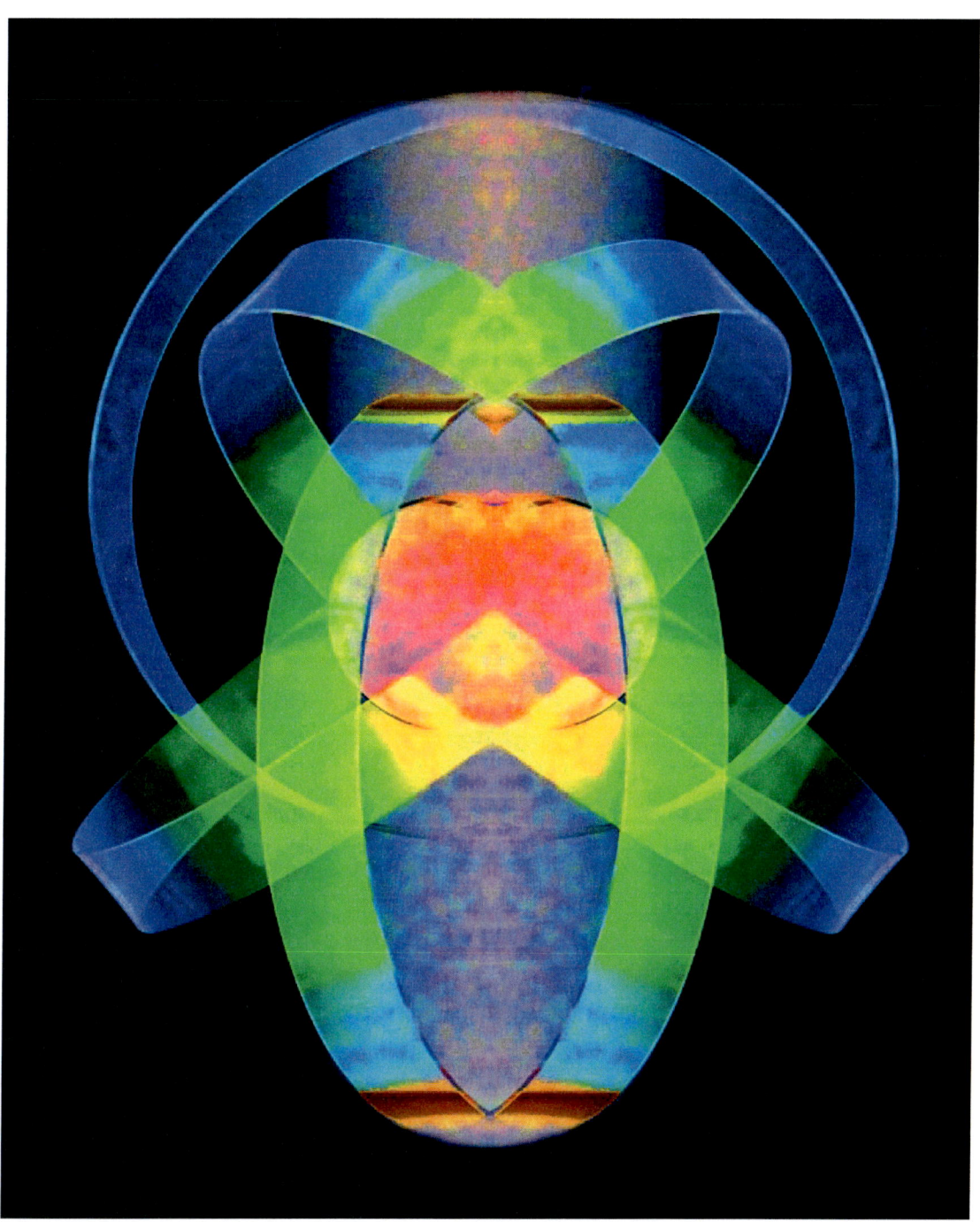

Minsky had the insight to say "The principal activities of the brains are making changes in themselves".

Is all our Life, then but a dream
Seen faintly in the golden gleam
Athwart Time's dark resistless stream?

LEWIS CARROLL, Sylvie and Bruno.

TIME, SPACE and CHAOS with these subjects, we will eventually recognise the pattern of understanding human existence.

She told me "He is smarter than he looks." My biggest fear is that eventually you will see me the way I see myself.

There is no existence except in the thoughts of the human mind.....

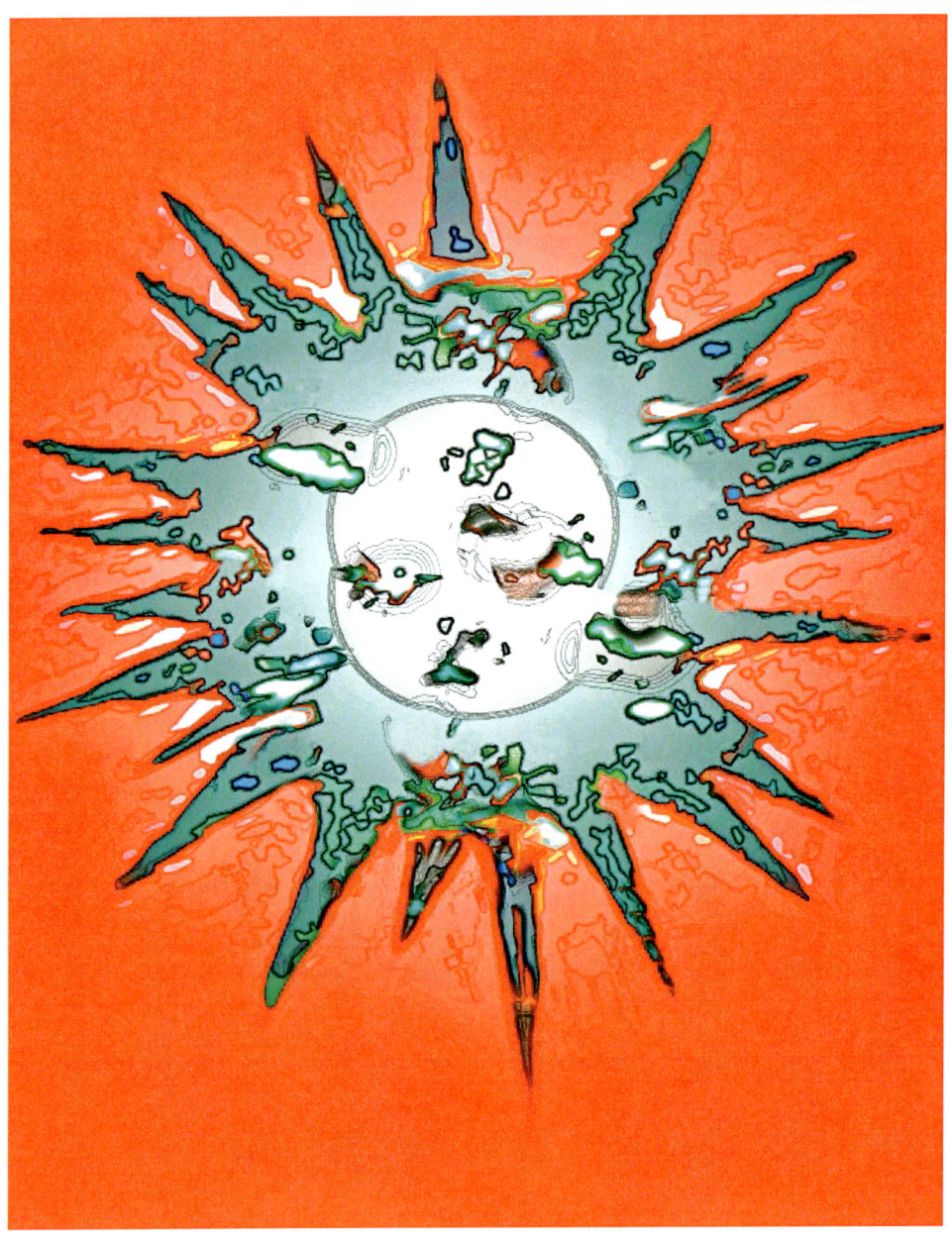

Creative problem solving is shared by scientists and artists.....
These are some of the tools for thinking which are most commonly used for creativity; pattern forming, empathising, modelling, transforming, synthesising, imaging, abstract conception, observing and dimensional thinking.

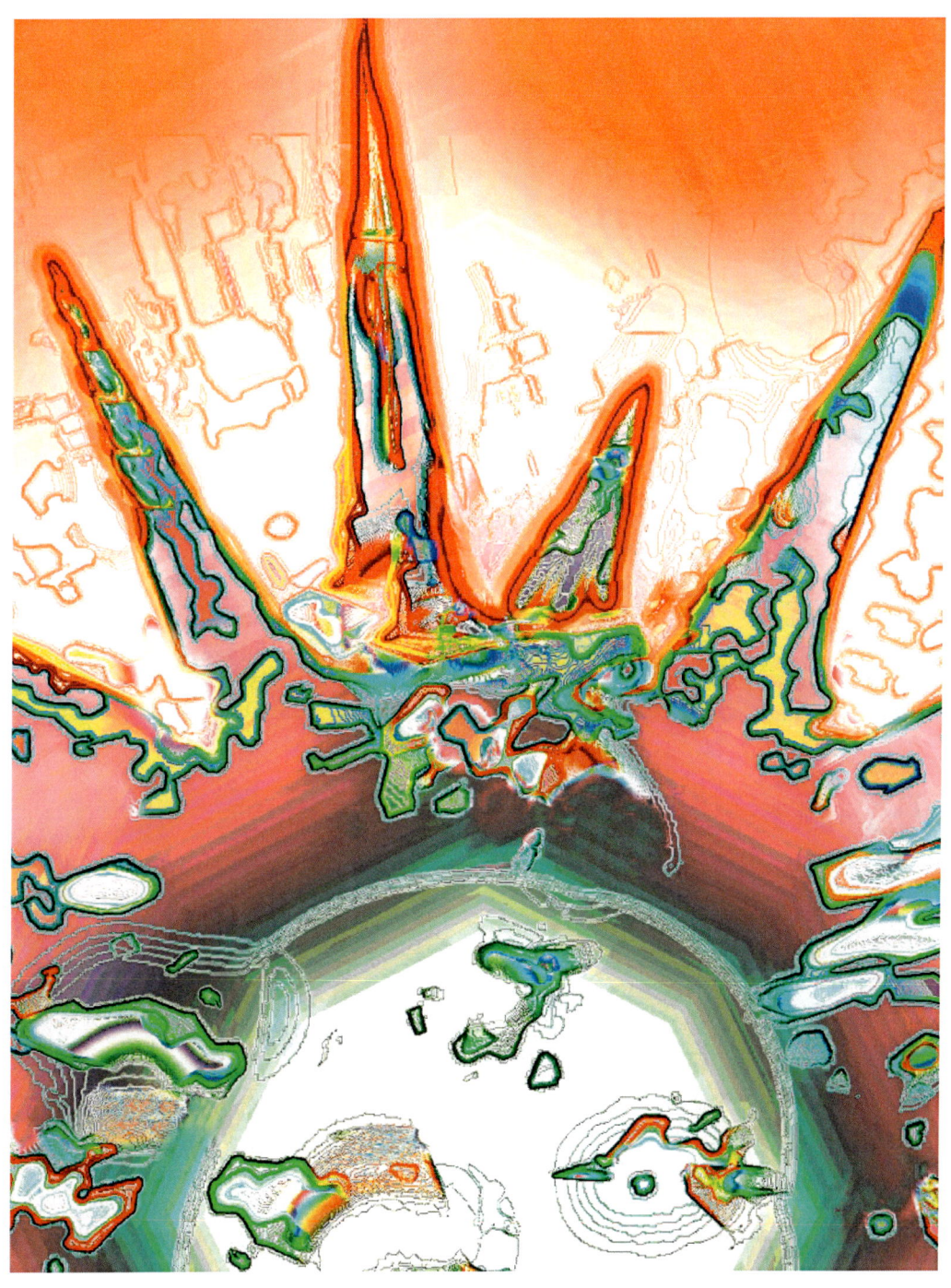

In the future looking at art will be taken as pills.....
See page 50.....On the left 206 the whole picture!

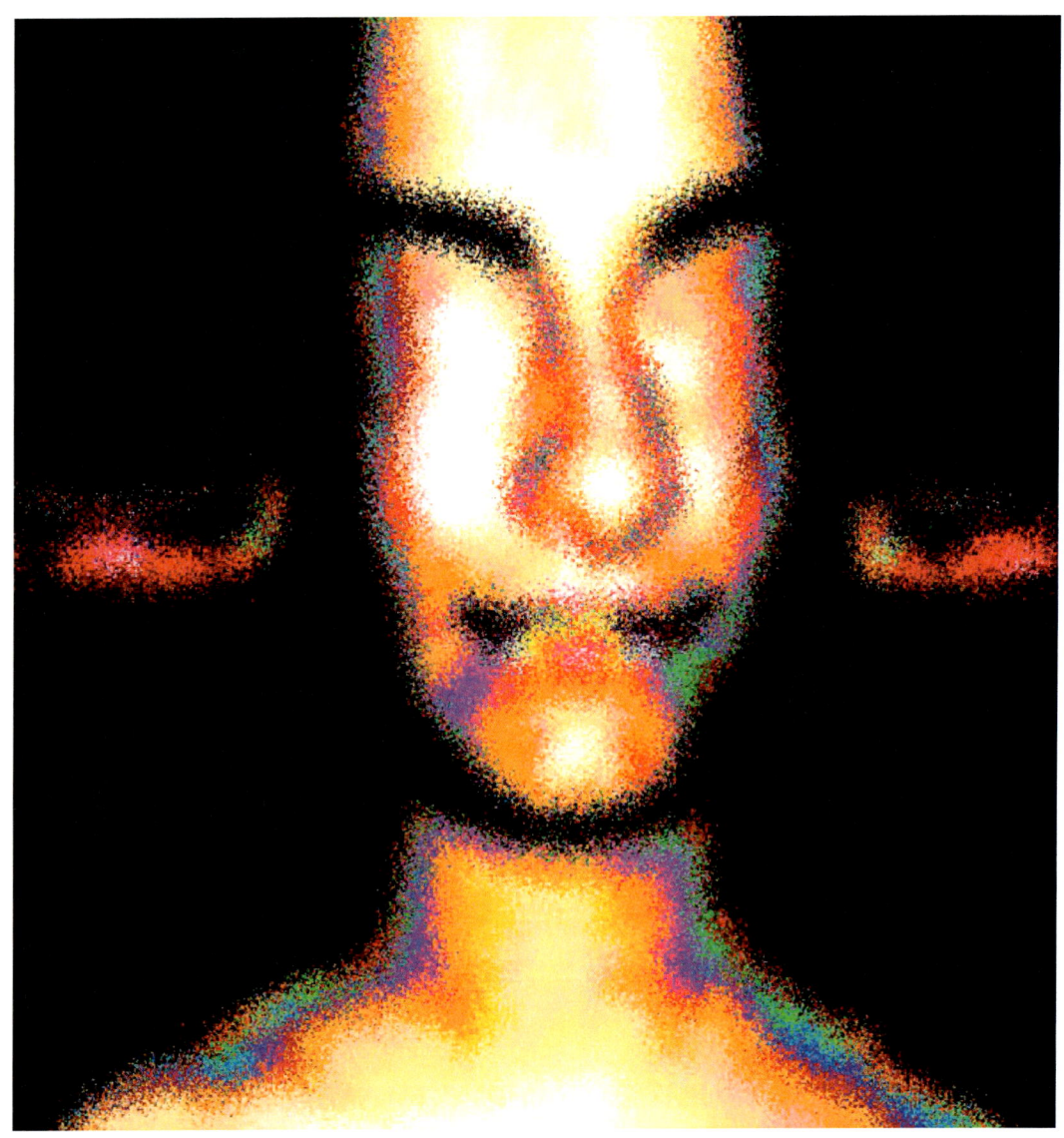

Though no one can go back and make a brand new start,
anyone can start from now and make a brand new ending.

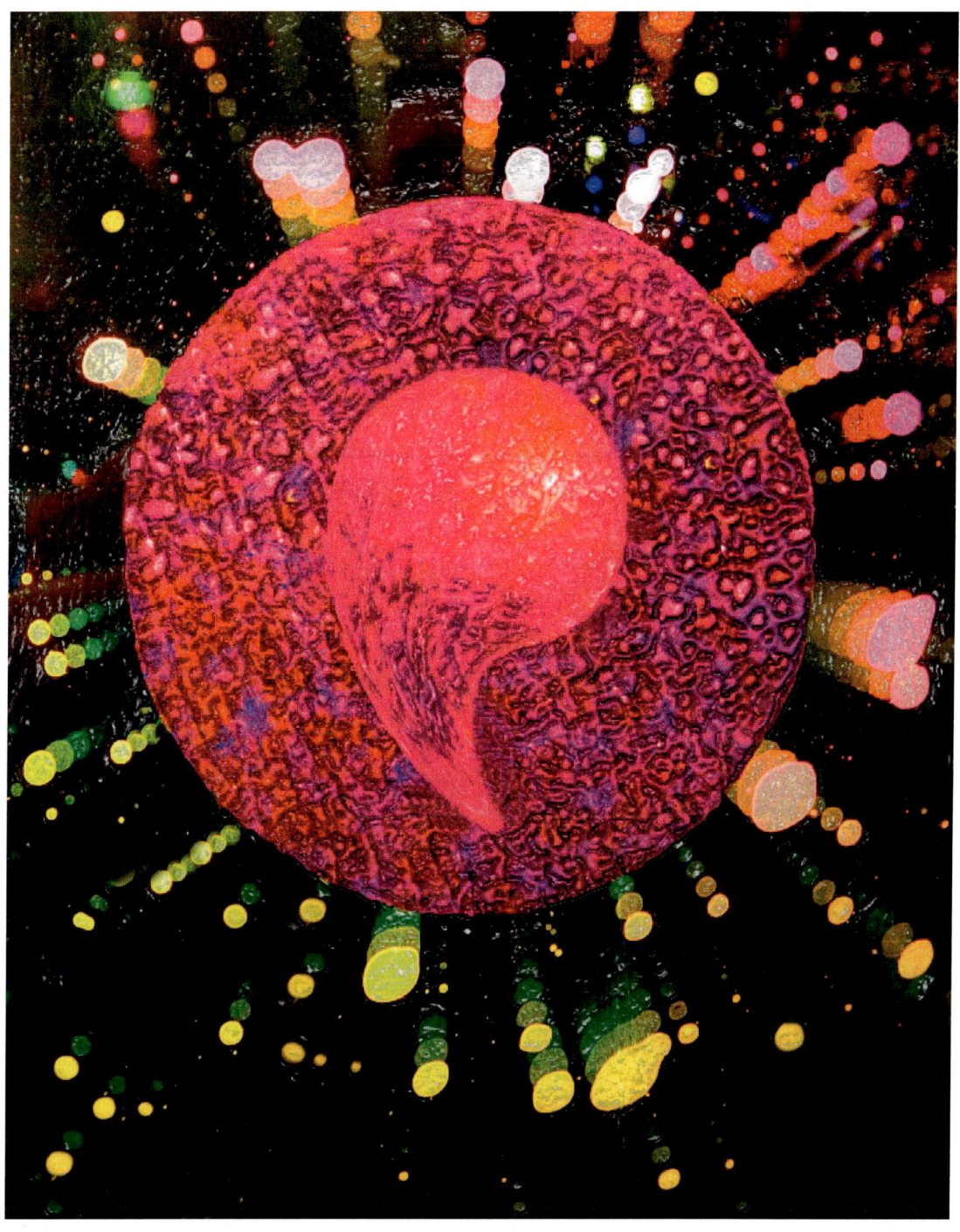

The essential ingredient for creativity is wasting time.....Right.....Goals determine your thoughts.....Thoughts determine your life.

Art is rarely created in a moment of inspiration, there are so many thoughts, experiences, and influences that drive the artist to his work.

I travel not to escape life, but for life not to escape me.....
When you go through The Rockies you really have come to the mountain!

Bubblewrap, what a pin prick.....I bet he goes to bed with a book!

One day you'll look forward to waking up in the morning. I promise.

PTSD don't cry for me Sargentina.

Our weapons don't work.....Software encryption PGP.....This has to be a software issue with the intell human genome! I worked with the second gen intercourse engine before, and this reacts like an artifact when the packet alignment bytes are wrong or out of sync, and the compression algorithm compensates for this by just interpolating the signal. However, signals are very lossy, something around the -85% chaos quantum rate. This means there's a lot of garbage that needs to be filtered out, most of it done in software. I think that the manual router is just not doing its job right, and that is what is causing the reproduction failure in 21st century people.

If we kill them can we have it all. You know your time is running out!

When I touched the face of god there was balance and rising synthesis.....

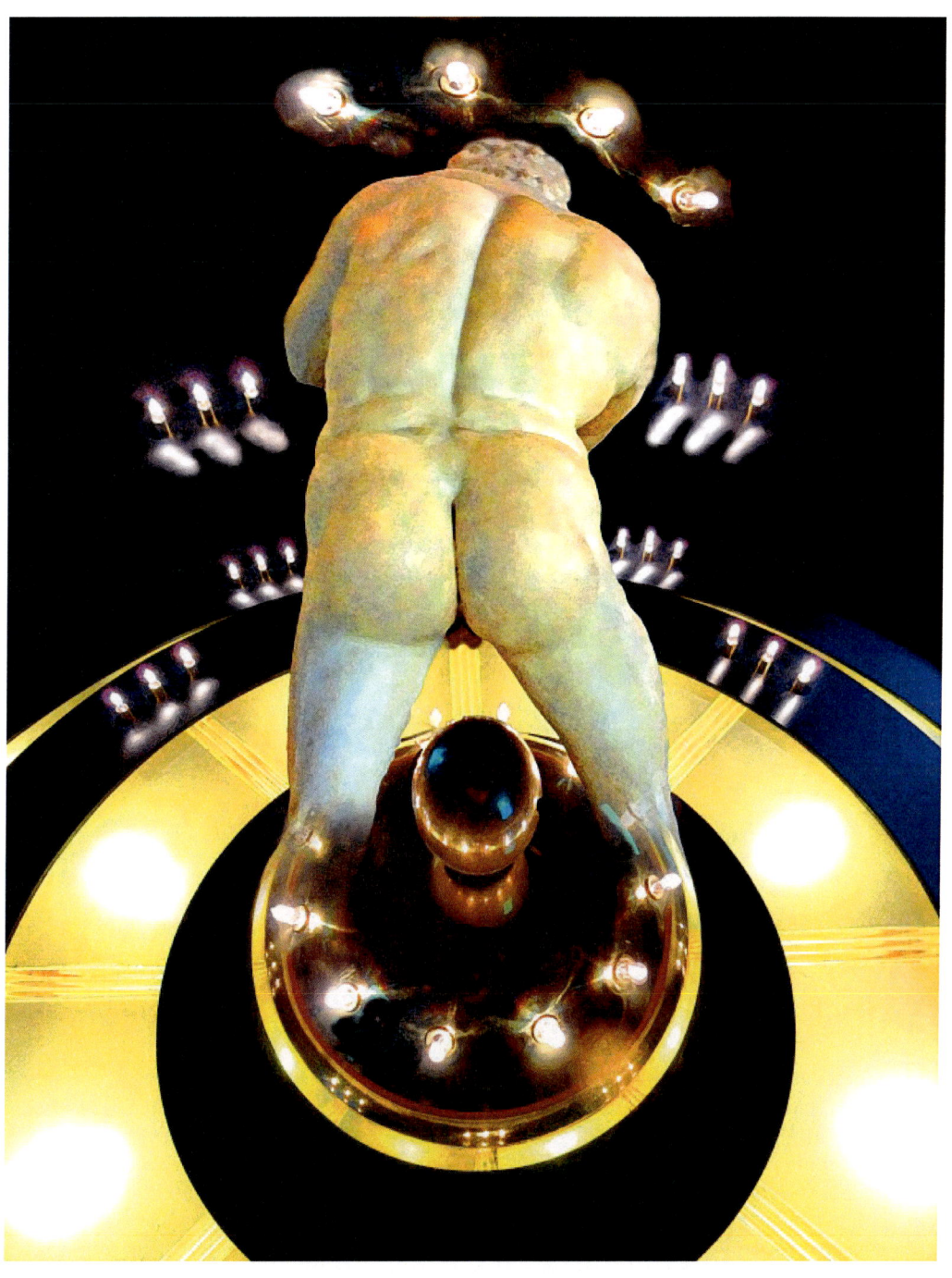

There is no need to kill people for their human organs on demand. Now you can go to the labs and they will create a new liver for you in 24 hours at a cost of $923.

There is currently no known cure for life.....It is a sexually transmitted disease which always ends in death. His brains are where?

The idea of loving a robot may seem strange or even totally wrong. Through history our opinions of what is morally acceptable have changed constantly..... Do you love your phone computer companion. Time will change us.

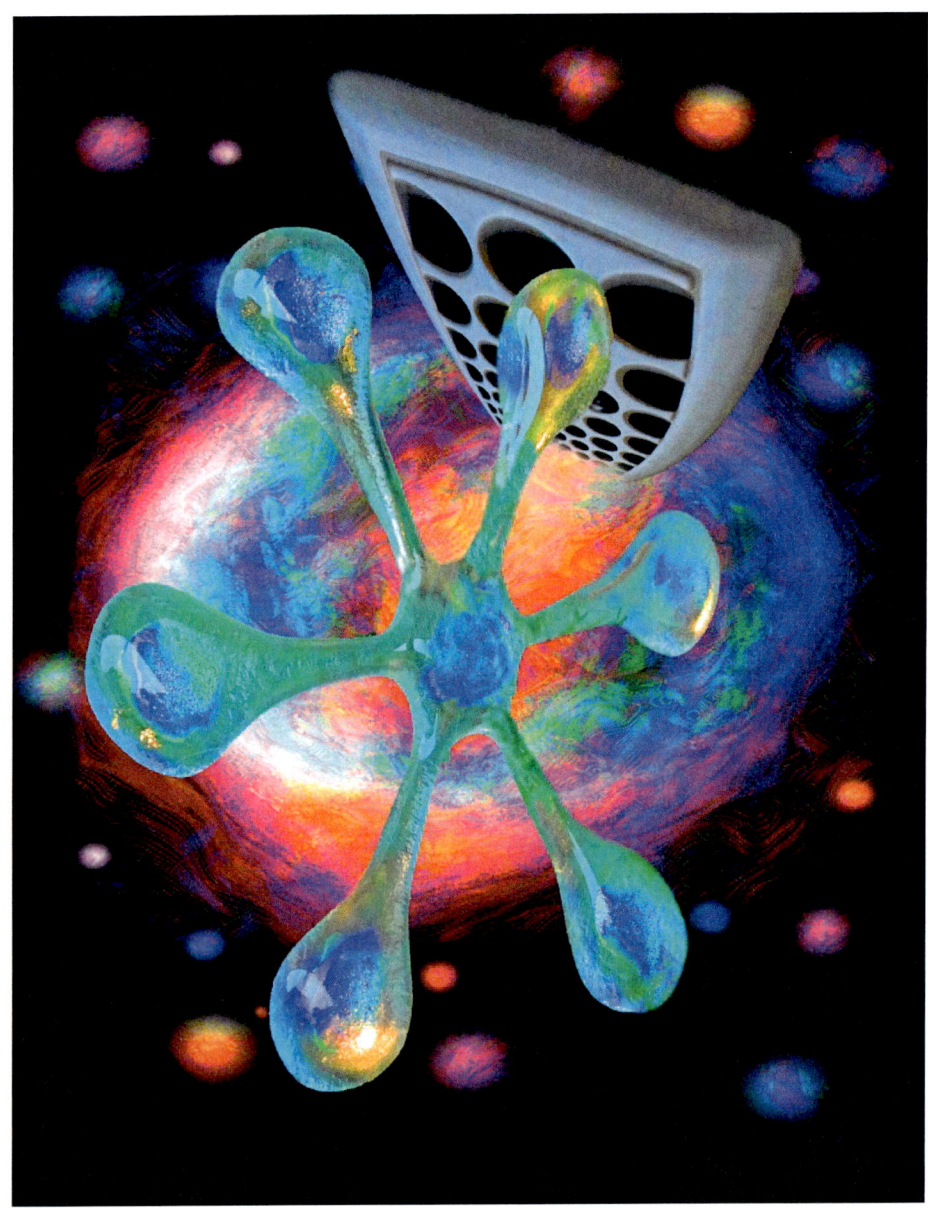

You know sometimes you feel like quitting, well that is the time to think about why you started.....

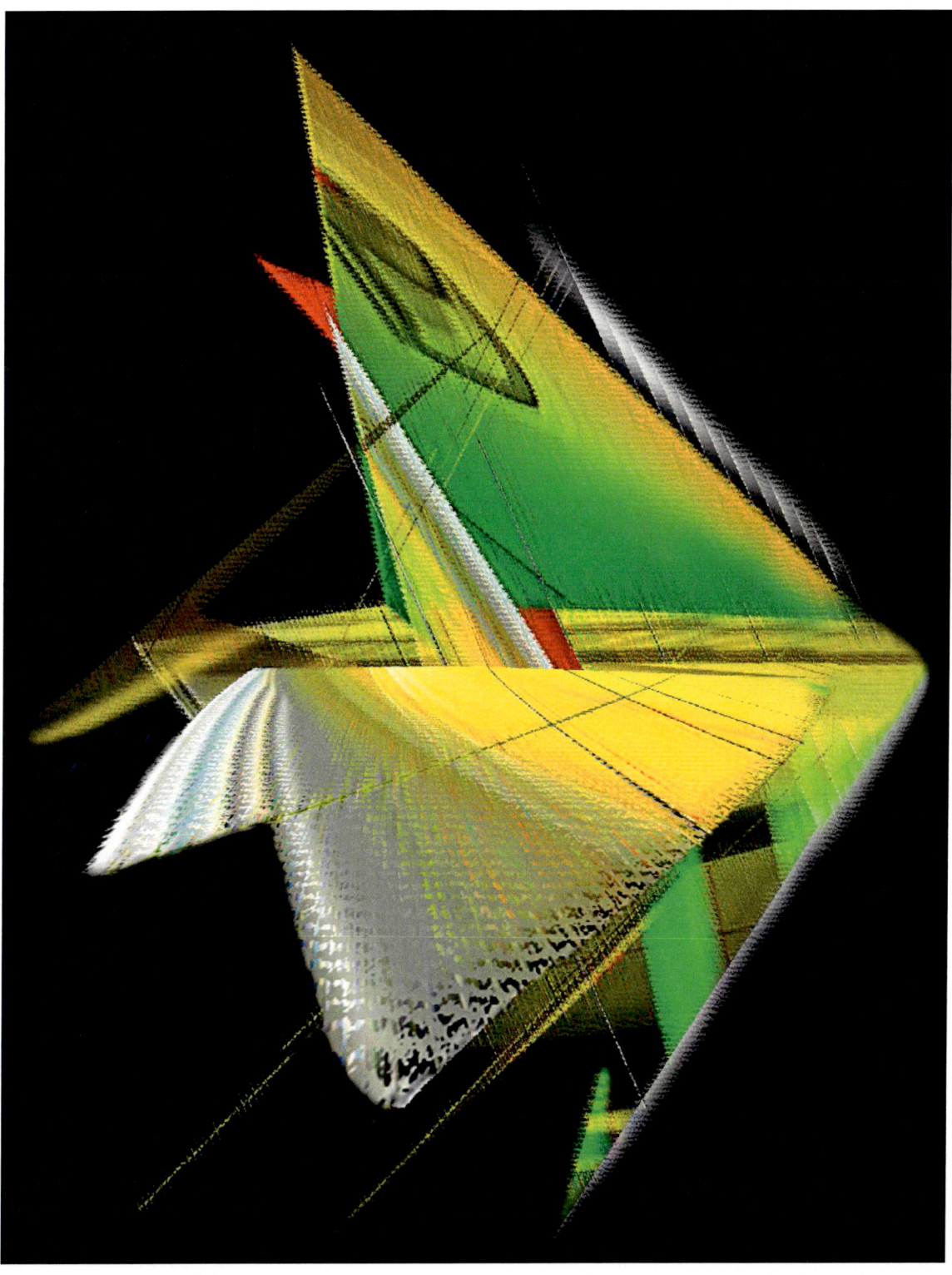

Look! A space butterfly.....What you expect from love and life sometimes does not happen.

We all create our own small worlds around us, so we can have control and routine in our entire existense.

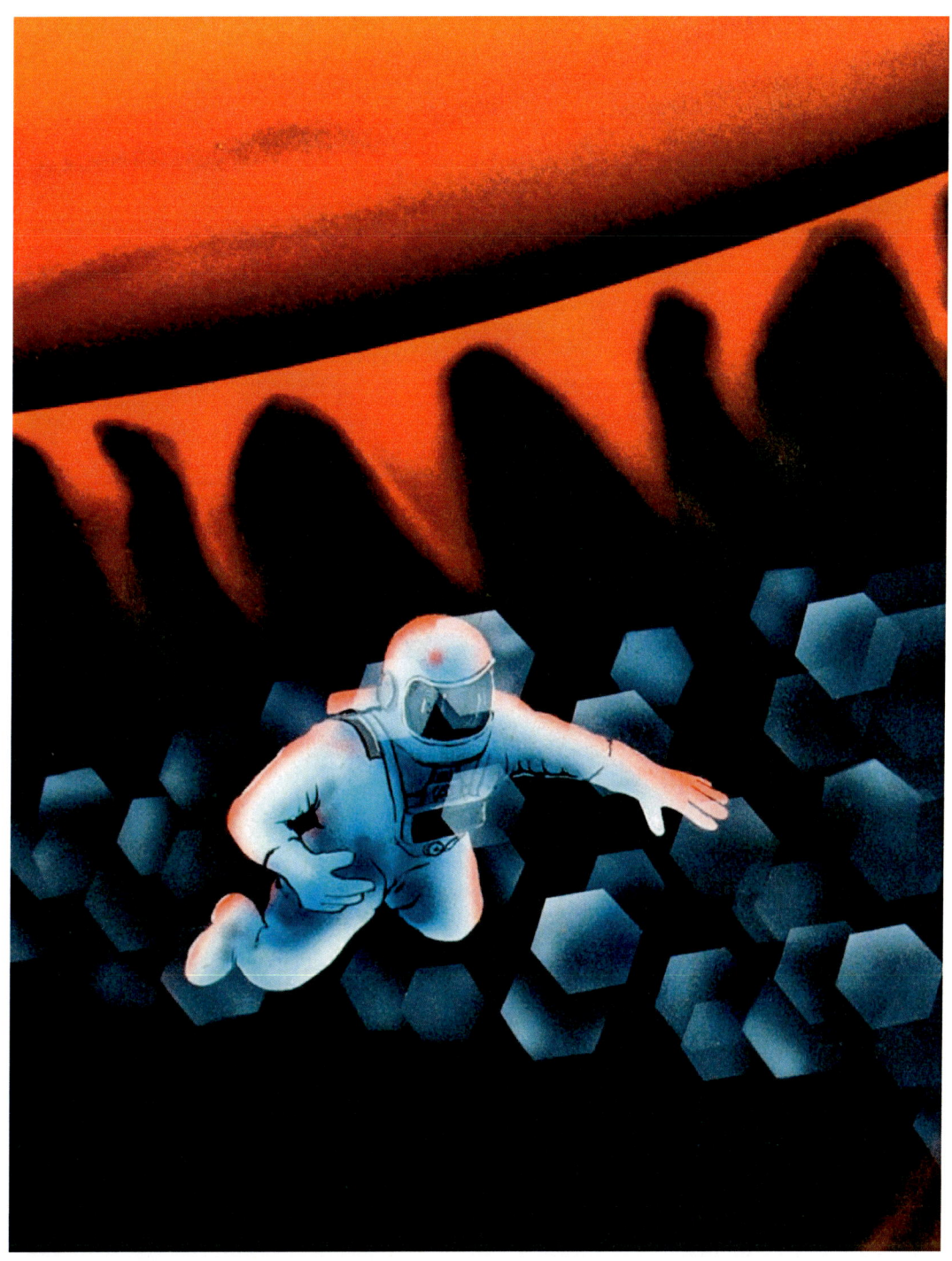

Where are the pigs in space? All life on this planet is made from the same substance, and why are we more creative and intelligent than pigs?

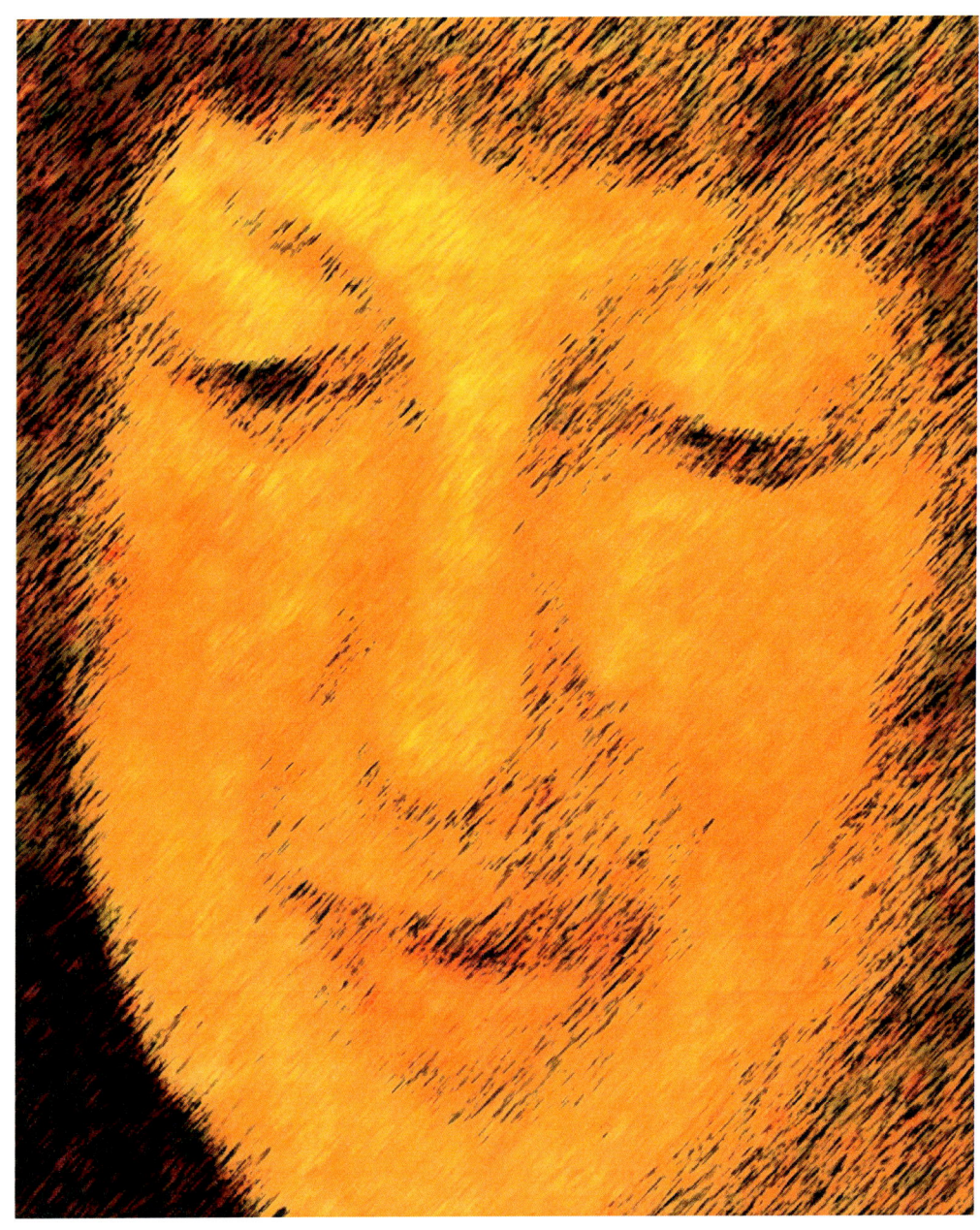

You are as young as your smile.....But we are controlled by our genetic code, our survival is created by social cooperation.

At the moment at least my thoughts are still my own and private.....My skin is showing its age!
I have a serious case of chronic progressive decrepitude.....

On a pay phone: don't have phone sex – you might get hearing Aids!
Today I must reinvent myself again and learn how to code while listening to bangla.

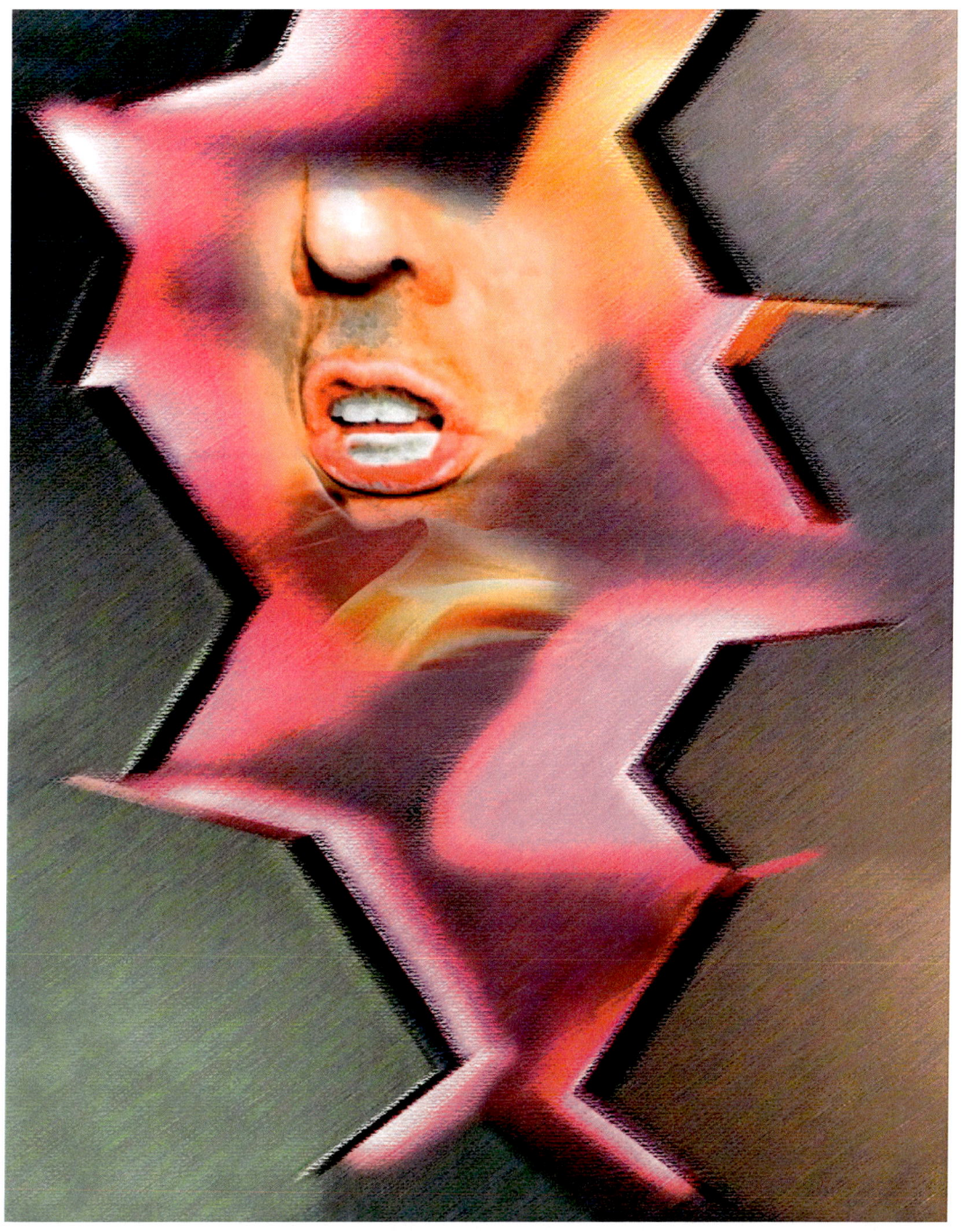

Reflections and rejections are yesterday's sad memories. Road rage says it all! I am fearfull of where society is going.....

My everyday is a gradual process of inner change depending on my ears, eyes, phages and people around me.....

130 million new humans every year.....In 1965 those who were
a bit trippy are now the establishment. Happy days!

With every rising Tuscan sun, think eating, and your life has just begun.

I get out of my art what I am willing to give up for it.

We should be aware of our "present moment" instead of losing ourselves in worry and anxiety about the future or the past.

We eat Pigs, little Lambs, Dogs. Dolphins, Whales, Fish, Horses, Cows and, of course, there is always Broccoli.....

Turn over a new leaf instead of looking back at the signs of aging and decay.....

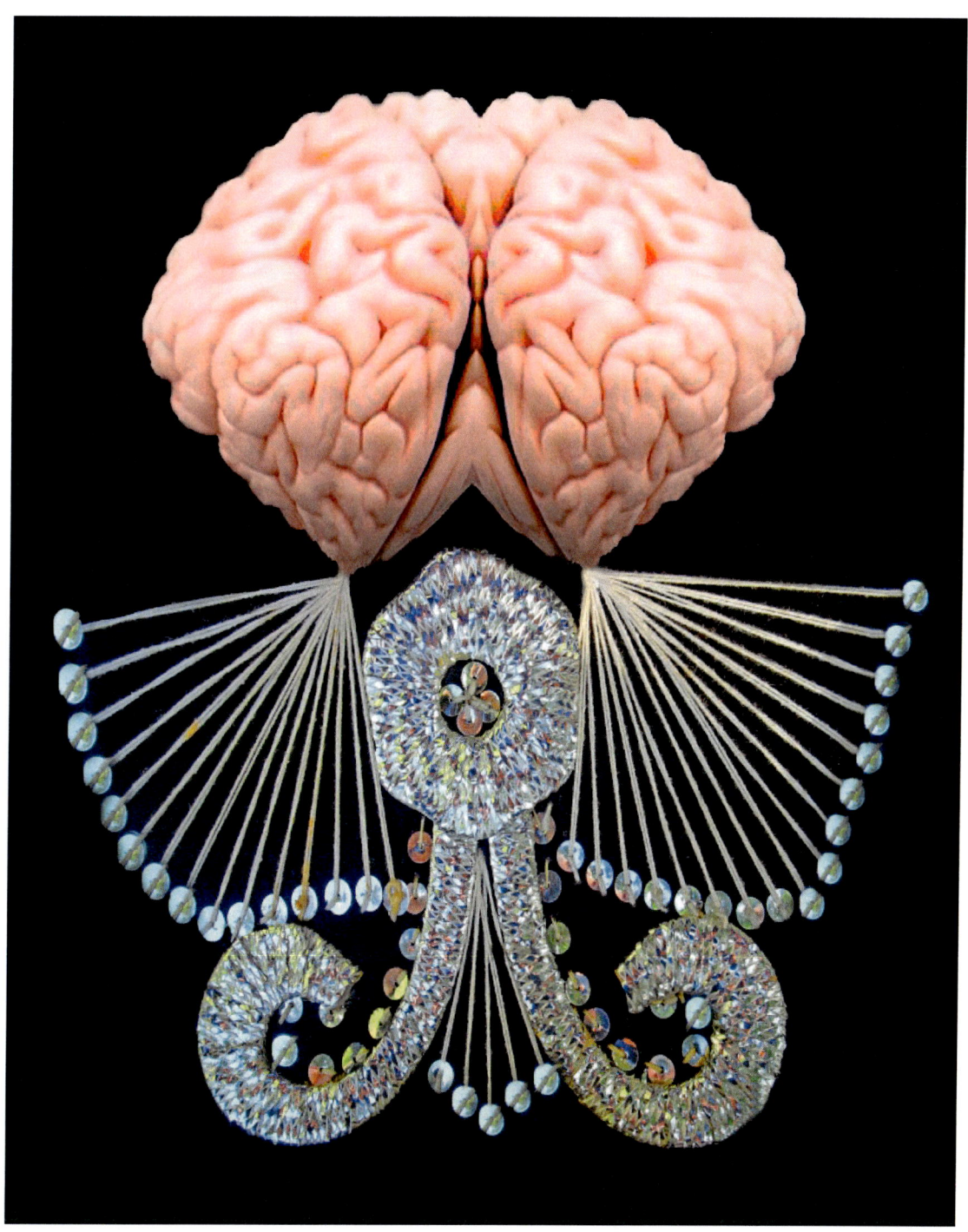

My friends in Singapore have just had a DNA gene transplant, and the result is they will never get 423 types of cancer ever.

When something great happens I wake up.
Then again everyday works for somebody!

Jon Jetson says "People may doubt what you say, but they will believe what you do."

Making love is a gaia artistic earthy sensation caused by sensual temptation, when a man puts his primal location in a woman's exotic destination. Did you understand the visual explanation shown in this painting or would you like a demonstration?

Oh Canada.....there are no shortcuts to any place worth going to.

Snowden told us….."Smartphone users can do very little to stop security services getting control over their devices."

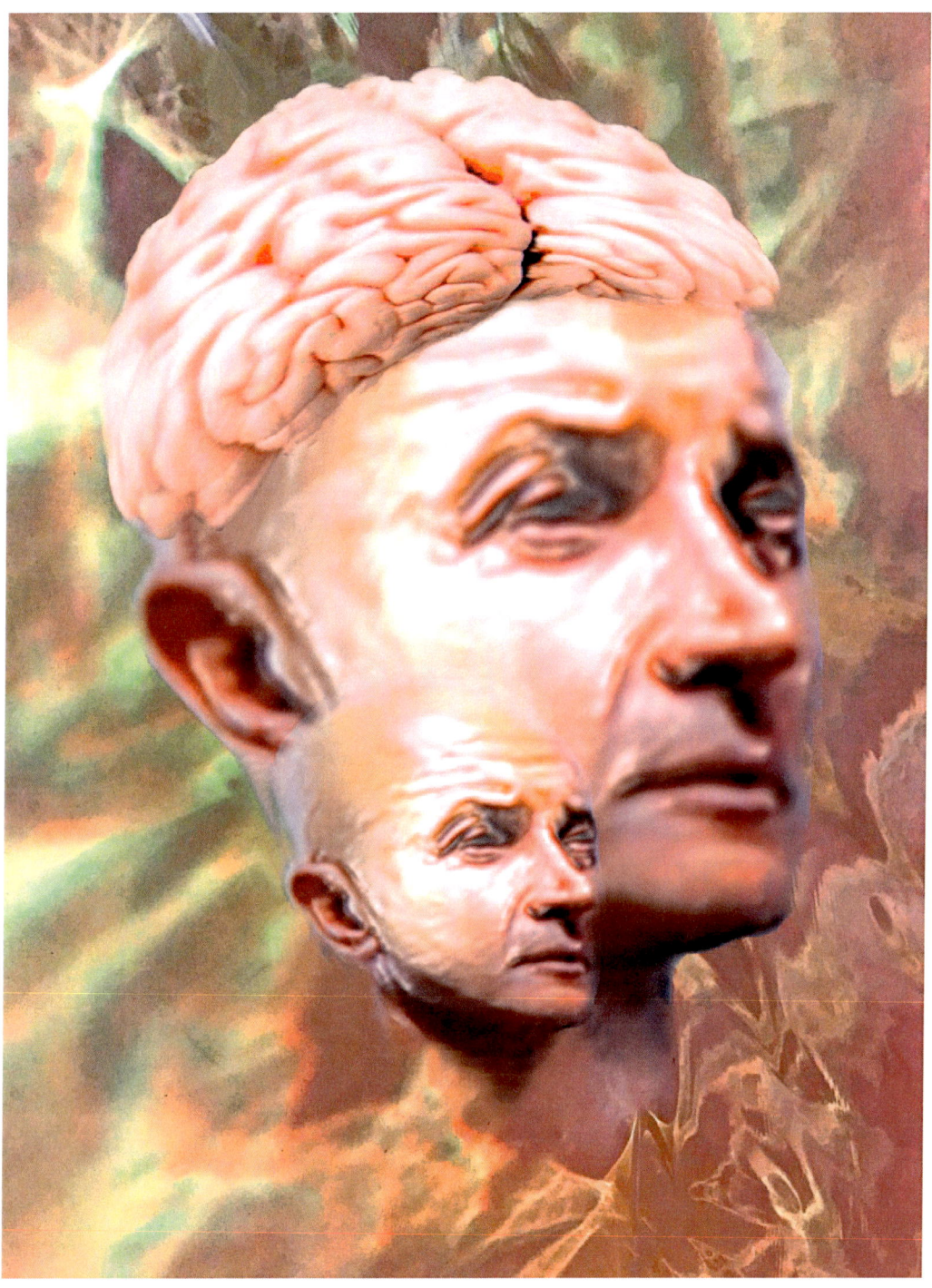

Since Huxley the pharmaceutical industry has pursued making money out of the biochemical pursuit of happiness.....1 billion people spending billions and billions on drugs that make them able to cope with their daily lives, all searching for happiness.

Consciousness: That annoying time between sleep.

Looking out across Como I should have remembered, love is the triumph of imagination over intelligence.

Please let me replace my reality with illusion.....I really like watching, I am not sure I like being!

Life today lives in the forest of mental madness, turmoil, broken routine, anger, pain and we just have to find a rock to crawl under and be comfortable.

Kabat-Zinn said this is it, really this is it. This is all there is!

These paintings only exist when you look at them.

I would love to know what people are thinking in the gallery, when they are looking at my paintings.

Art is long, life is short. Right Conrad.....All we have are our memories.....FREEEXIT, LIFES EXIT.....What matters? All ownership and feelings are gone.....

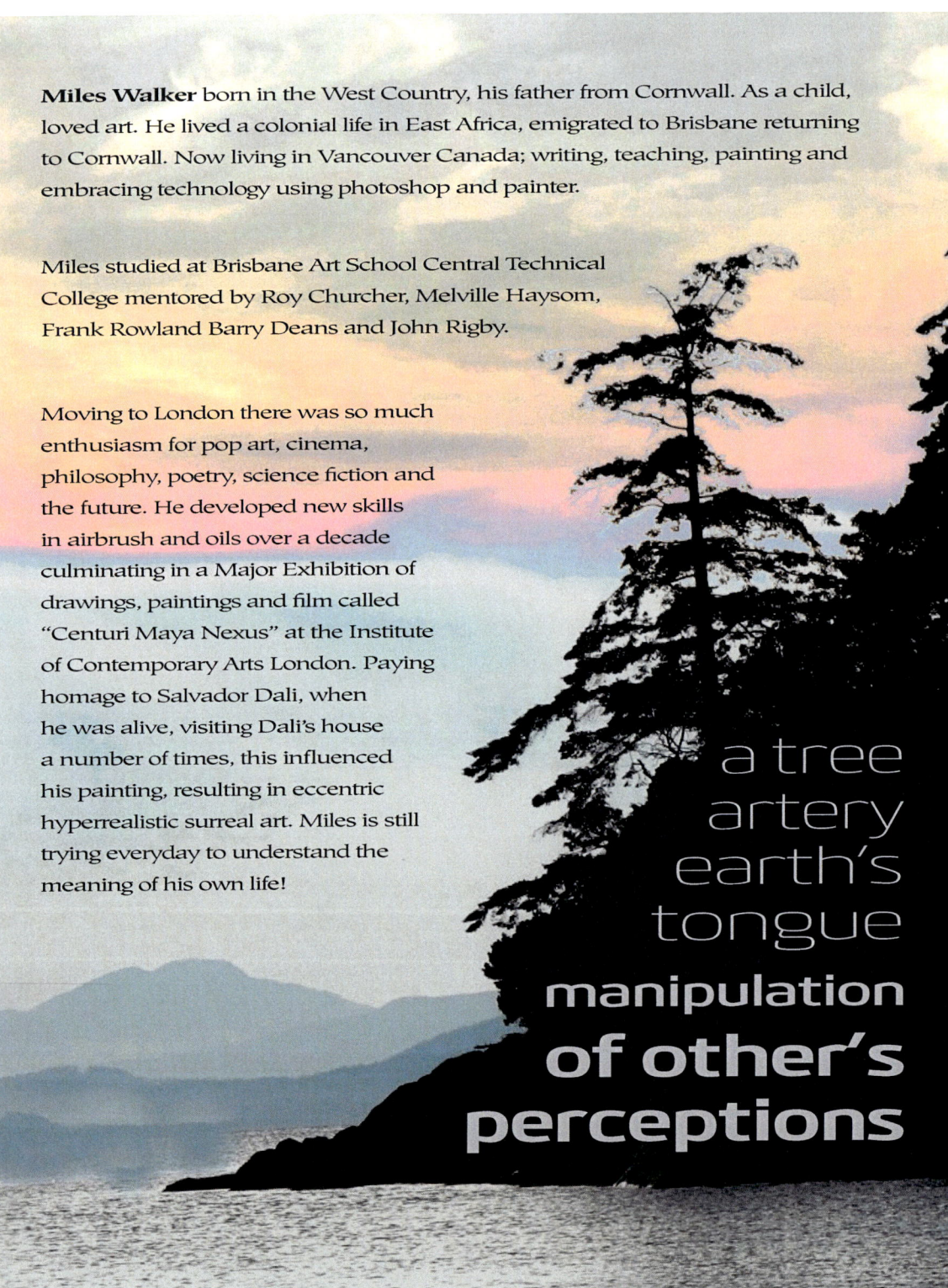

Miles Walker born in the West Country, his father from Cornwall. As a child, loved art. He lived a colonial life in East Africa, emigrated to Brisbane returning to Cornwall. Now living in Vancouver Canada; writing, teaching, painting and embracing technology using photoshop and painter.

Miles studied at Brisbane Art School Central Technical College mentored by Roy Churcher, Melville Haysom, Frank Rowland Barry Deans and John Rigby.

Moving to London there was so much enthusiasm for pop art, cinema, philosophy, poetry, science fiction and the future. He developed new skills in airbrush and oils over a decade culminating in a Major Exhibition of drawings, paintings and film called "Centuri Maya Nexus" at the Institute of Contemporary Arts London. Paying homage to Salvador Dali, when he was alive, visiting Dali's house a number of times, this influenced his painting, resulting in eccentric hyperrealistic surreal art. Miles is still trying everyday to understand the meaning of his own life!

a tree
artery
earth's
tongue
manipulation
of other's
perceptions

Made in the USA
San Bernardino, CA
23 May 2019